RS
FORDS
IN · COLOUR

RS
FORDS
IN · COLOUR
Escort · Capri · Sierra · Fiesta

EDITOR   *DENNIS FOY*

WINDROW & GREENE

Published in Great Britain 1991 by
Windrow & Greene Ltd
5 Gerrard Street
London W1V 7LJ

British Library Cataloguing in Publication Data
Foy, Dennis
 RS Fords in colour: Escort,. Capri, Sierra, Fiesta.
 I. Title
 629.2222

ISBN 1-872004-71-7

Additional design and production: *ghk* Design

Printed in Hong Kong

CONTENTS

Acknowledgements

This collection of RS Ford features which have appeared in issues of Performance Ford would not have been possible without a considerable degree of help, in particular from the owners of the various examples used to illustrate each feature. I would like to thank each of them again for their co-operation during photographic sessions — not all of which happened on calm, still, sunny days.

Then there are others who helped, during the research phase of each feature. As well as the owners, there were such people as Barry Reynolds, Don Hume and Steve Woolmington of Ford of Britain, the teams at Ford Motorsport and at Special Vehicle Engineering, and Dan Frazer and Sheila Knapman of Ford Photographic Unit.

Also singled out for thanks is my wife Pat, who has patiently ensured that Performance Ford invariably goes together as it ought to each month, despite the fact that I spend too long talking cars with just about anybody who owns an interesting RS Ford.

Finally, there are two companies who have helped considerably with the production of these specific features: Sarah Curl Phototypesetting, and Denton Repro, who between them ensured that what I intended to appear on each page actually did appear, just as I hoped. And, quite often, better than I dared hope.

Thanks, all of you.

Dennis Foy,   July 1991

Introduction — "A breed apart"

RS. Two little letters which, in bald acronymical terms, stand for Rallye Sport — but which to the aficionado mean more. Much more.

Despite its awesome bulk and scale of operations, the Ford Motor Company has proved through the range of RS cars which it has developed — mostly in Britain, but sometimes in Germany — that it is capable of providing exciting cars along with the hundreds of thousands of ordinary, transportation-for-the-masses machines which are churned out of its factories across Europe each year.

In all but two cases (the RS1700T and the RS200 which followed several years later) the RS models featured in this collection have evolved from more mundane models with which they have continued to share the bodyshell, quite a number of the mechanical components, and many of the trim pieces. Yet, in every case, the RS model has stood head-and-shoulders above its stablemates.

So what sets them apart?

There have been two names which have interwoven with the RS-badged products, neither of which has ever been formally part of the mighty Ford empire. The first was Lotus, whose peppy twin overhead camshaft engine was used initially in the car which started the RS revolution (the Cortina Lotus brought with it the need for a specialised, dedicated dealer network within the main dealer structure), and then came a far more enduring connection: Cosworth.

Founded by Mike Costin and Keith Duckworth in 1958, Cosworth Engineering's first acknowledged direct engineering involvement with Ford's British division came in the early sixties, when they were invited to tune the overhead valve 1.5 litre engine used in the MkI Cortina. The company remained associated with Ford for almost a decade after that, again working quietly and virtually uncredited, except by those in the know. But suddenly in the early seventies their name rose to prominence when it was acknowledged as being responsible for the wonderful sixteen valve twin-cam engine beneath the bonnet of the RS1600 MkI Escort.

This engine had been developed by Cosworth and was essentially a completely new head on a Ford Kent crossflow cylinder block. That Ford had already experienced a tremendous level of Formula One success with a Cosworth-developed V8 engine (the DFV had achieved the status of instant legend when Jim Clark won the 1967 Dutch Grand Prix at Zandvoort, first time out) doubtless enhanced Cosworth's chances of gaining Original Equipment status for their 1600cc DOHC engine (the BDA, which stands for Belt Driven series A); but what undeniably clinched the deal was that the powerplant was stunningly effective. The BDA served Ford well, helping the works team, and countless privateers, to win an awesome number of races and rallies throughout two generations of Escort.

In the seventies Zakspeed had encouraged Cosworth to look into turbocharging, and from that programme came the legendary silhouette Capris which did much to enhance that model's image in Germany. That turbo-charged engine was developed still further and by process of evolution was used in the RS1700T, then the RS200, and, in its latest YBF form, the four generations of Sierra Cosworth. Whilst there are no parts interchangeable between those early BDAs and the latest versions of the turbocharged Cosworth twin-cam, the lineage is acknowledged by all concerned.

Yet there is much more to the RS than just the engine. To me, effective and impressive as the engine in any RS might be, the one single factor which sticks in my mind when reflecting on an RS model is the feedback which the driver gains. This usually takes the form of a 'tingle', a special feel which is uniquely Rallye Sport in character.

Although there is not a single person who has been involved in the RS programme right from Day One (the Cortina Lotus was developed by Lotus Cars, and Sam Toy's RS dealership was created at the same time as the first examples went on sale in 1963), that special RS feel has always been there. Whether it is a Cortina Lotus, an RS1600, an RS2000 MkII or the very latest Sierra Sapphire RS Cosworth 4x4, the feeling that the driver matters is a constant feature.

Which in itself is fascinating, for the cars were developed in a variety of different ways in a variety of different locations throughout the Ford empire. The RS1600, for example, was developed at Ford's Competitions Department in Essex, whilst the RS1600i which came two generations later was a Merkenich product, and the entire range of turbocharged production cars was put together by the Special Vehicle Engineering team at Dunton, Ford's research and development facility near Southend-on-Sea. One or two of the cars were almost 'let's see if it can be done' efforts by a small team of enthusiasts working outside the main Ford infrastructure, whilst others were major, approved-from-the-top-floor projects with pre-production schedules and budgets. For each and every model to come out with a distinctive, common feel — that tingle I mentioned earlier — is a major achievement.

During my long, and usually pleasant, association with the Ford Motor Company, I have enjoyed the privilege of meeting, talking with, getting to know, many of the prime movers who were responsible for the RS cars. And without exception, from the very top to the most junior employee, they have been enthusiasts.

Sam Toy, for example, will always be remembered for his favouring of nippy, fun cars — and had it not been for him and his infectious enthusiasm, it is highly unlikely that there would today be such a thriving RS network. His reason for establishing the sub-network was a sensible one: the Cortina Lotus was a thoroughbred requiring a level of service and sales back-up which was some way above the standards then extant within the main dealer-ship structure. However, once it was in place, Sam was astute enough to realise that there was a special type of customer emerging, and that in turn paved the way for more cars with the same character as the Lotus-developed product.

Then there was the entire team at the old Competitions Department, each and every one of whom was seriously into building winning cars. Although motorsport-led, their products were often translated into road cars. Although none of them ever really thought in terms of high build numbers, their ability to create something special from a package of readily-available components was instrumental in assuring the production viability of the various models they developed.

And, of course, there is the team at SVE. Established in 1980 as a facility for trouble-shooting, for finding solutions which would be beyond the scope of any conventional R & D department because of the complexity and time-consuming nature of special projects, SVE is staffed — and has been from the very beginning —with highly-qualified engineers who are, to a man, committed both professionally and personally to 'driver's cars'. Products such as the Escort RS Turbo, and the Sierra and Sapphire Cosworths, prove my point. All of those cars are driving machines — built by enthusiasts for enthusiasts.

The owners of RS cars are a breed apart. The cars with that prefix to their name are rarely bought by drivers who do not appreciate the nature of the beast, and this is proved by two thriving owners' clubs. The AVO OC looks after all models built at the old Aveley site, whilst the RSOC sees its remit as maintaining links between all owners of Rallye Sport cars.

A peculiarity of the RS range is that it has never caught on anywhere else but Britain as a marketing tool: only this country has a dedicated dealership network. Yet in spite of this apparent suppression by Ford, RS cars are in demand throughout the world — most conspicuously in Australia, where certain models were imported in kit form in the seventies and where the following is as strong now as it is in Britain.

The RS marque has been threatened from time to time, especially when new blood has moved into the spacious, quiet calm of Ford of Britain's headquarters in Warley, Essex — in particular, to the seclusion of the top floor, which is where the directors have their offices and boardroom. But every time that there has been the idea of doing away with the RS name, it has met with stiff resistance, especially from street level. Long may it reign!

CORTINA LOTUS

The car that started the RS revolution

That Ford could ever market a version of their new mid-sized car which features a sophisticated twin-cam engine and a maximum speed comfortably in excess of "the ton" was almost inconceivable back in 1962. Yet a year later they did just that, producing (with more than a little help from sportscar manufacturer Lotus) the all-conquering Cortina Lotus.

Credit for the concept must be lain at the feet of Walter Hayes, presently Vice-Chairman of Ford of Europe, but back in 1962 a newly-arrived member of the Ford Public Affairs Department. Anxious to capitalise on the marketing potential of having Ford cars prominent on Britain's racetracks and rallies, Walter Hayes got in touch with his old friend Colin Chapman, whose Lotus company were already producing their own version of the engine which would power the as-yet-unannounced Cortina range. This engine, which topped the block of the Ford product with a twin-cam cylinder head produced by Lotus to designs by one Harry Mundy, was able to pump out more than 100 b.h.p. — no mean achievement at the time.

Hayes reasoned that combining the two elements — Chapman's engine and Ford's new car — would be a surefire winner in competition, and Colin Chapman was not inclined to disagree. Thus, having agreed terms by the middle of 1962, Lotus were left to it to not only develop the project, but to make deliveries of the first batch by the beginning of 1963.

The car was known within Lotus as the Type 28, and the method of production chosen by Ford was that Lotus would be supplied at their Cheshunt factory with two-door Cortina bodyshells, and a short time later would receive back complete cars, which Ford could market through their dealer network. The first stage of conversion, or more accurately of building up the shells into cars, was to install the 1558cc (125E) engine, which was backed up with the all-synchromesh gearbox of the Lotus Elan, the two components being joined by a specially-cast aluminium clutch housing. These two components fit into the shell without any difficulty, thanks to the generous amounts of space available within the Cortina's engine bay.

Next, Lotus got to work on the rear suspension system of the original Cortina, and developed their own, far more substantial and sporting, axle location system. This involved replacing the original equipment leaf springs of the Ford with a set of coil springs, mounting to the axle via a set of specially-designed brackets. These spring units had internal dampers, and the original damper top-mounts were used to locate the new spring and damper units of the Lotus development. Next, a pair of trailing arms from the original car's leaf spring forward pickup

points to the axle were installed. Finally, an "A" frame was installed, with its apex locating onto the specially-modified differential casing, and its open ends bracketed to the floorpan close to the radius arm pickup points. To ensure that all remained as solid as the designer intended, stiffening tubes were strategically affixed around the rear floorpan of the car.

The front suspension came in for attention also, but not on anything like as grand a scale afforded to the rear. Shorter struts with uprated damping were installed, along with a set of lower, stiffer springs than those found on any other model of Cortina. Forged track control arms were fitted, and a faster (3.0 turns lock-to-lock, as opposed to the usual 4.2) steering box was installed. The braking system was specified at 9.5" front discs

with 9" x 1¾" rear drums, and the car was the only car in the range at the time to have the luxury of servo assistance.

Overall the car sat extremely low — lower, in fact, than any other Cortina ever has, in the showroom. Coupled with the wide steel wheels of 5.5" x 13" with their 6.0" crossplies, the car looked aggressive — an appearance emphasised by the frontal elevation of the Lotus Cortina, which used small quarter bumpers in place of the usual full-width blade affair.

Identifying the car was easy: they came in any colour you like, as long as it was white with a green sidestripe. Discreet Lotus rondels were affixed to each rear wing and to the front grille, but ▷

CORTINA LOTUS

there was no badging whatsoever on the rear of the car. The doorskins, bonnet and bootlid were in light alloy, which kept the weight of those early cars down to about 1700 lbs.

That the original intention of the Hayes/Chapman coalition was to score success on racetracks was immediately apparent upon looking inside the car; it was a bit basic, to say the least. The seats were rudimentary buckets in the front and a bench in the rear, all finished in black vinyl — as were the door liner panels. Ahead of the driver was a binnacle unique to this car which contained four clocks, and there was a wood-rimmed alloy steering wheel. The rest of it was a combination of much painted metal, a bit of padding, and the occasional strip of chromed trim.

But of course these cars were not about luxury — they were built to go, and go they certainly did. The engine was enough to endow the car with a power-to-weight ratio of more than 135 b.h.p./ton, and that is a figure which is creditable today, so

> "These cars were not about luxury. They were built to go, and go they certainly did."

back in 1963 it was revolutionary. The top speed of the car was put at about 105-110 m.p.h. depending on the output of that particular engine (they varied quite a bit ...), and acceleration from 0-60 m.p.h. could be as good as ten seconds dead. However, where the car really scored was not in sprinting from traffic lights, but in blasting through curving roads. There, it was almost inassailable with enough power available to push out the tail if too much throttle was applied, even at quite high cornering speeds.

The car could not only go through bends very rapidly and very safely — learn to handle the wayward rear and it was surprisingly

friendly towards the driver — but could also stop quickly and squarely, thanks to those big front discs. Steering weights were always good, and the inter-relationship between controls, both foot and hand, were excellent.

Unfortunately, those early cars also showed a tendency to damaging their own rear axles, and the close-ratio Elan box (a development of the Cortina unit) proved less-than-ideal in a car which weighed some 300 lbs more than the sportscar for which the gear clusters were chosen.

To overcome these problems, one or two revisions were introduced in the early part of 1964. These started with the Elan gearbox being dropped in favour of that of the GT Cortina for production cars — the original close-ratio item was still available for competition use — and this meant a change from cast alloy to cast iron for the casings. To overcome the problem of rear axle vibration, the original one-piece propellor shaft was changed for a two-piece shaft. Production costs too were being looked at more closely by this time, and the result of a cost-cutting exercise was that the light alloy body panels were ditched, and standard Ford steel pressings were employed. It was July 1964 by the time that these changes made their way through to dealership showrooms, and a couple of months later there were more changes to be found, this time inside the cabin of the car.

Ford had by this point developed the Aeroflow "eyeball vent" ventilation system for the entire Cortina range, and the system was introduced to the Lotus Cortina along with a more attractive six-clock dashboard layout.

▲The interior of this early example of the car shows the distinctive fascia arrangement — and the abundance of painted metal.

THE LOTUS CORTINA IN COMPETITION

The list of names who have driven Lotus Cortinas in competition reads almost like a "who's who" of British and Scandinavian motorsport. Jackie Stewart, Jim Clark, Sir John Whitmore, Vic Elford, Roger Clark, Bengt Soderstrom, Graham Hill, Gunnar Palm, are just some of the legends who have successfully piloted the cars to victory in a range of races and rallies.

For Britain the cars were prepared by either Boreham or Lotus Cars at Cheshunt, whilst in Europe they were prepared by Alan Mann Racing.

Examples of the car are still to be found on racetracks, where they compete in Classic Saloons. LCR Secretary David Missions' example, shown here in mid-bend with one front wheel in mid-air, is highly successful, still able to fend off all but the most powerful of V8-engined machines with ease.

▲An original ad from 1963. Notice how the Lotus name only appears later in the ad, the car being pushed as the Consul Cortina ...

Externally another minor change was instigated, with the original car's grille being widened to full-width. Fortunately for fans, those quarter bumpers were retained.

A year later, in the middle of 1965, came the most important change to the specification of the Lotus Cortina. That radical rear suspension system, with its links and coil-over-damper arrangement, was dropped in favour of the conventional "cart spring" system which was to be found under the rear end of the Cortina GT. This too had a pair of forward-reaching radius arms, but true devotees of the marque were still horrified, considering the move to be a penny-pinching exercise on the part of Ford. Be that as it may, the benefits in terms of longevity and reliability outweighed the disadvantages of losing the Lotus-designed rear end.

The last major change to the Lotus Cortina came in the October of that year, when the gearbox was again changed, this time for the Corsair 2000E's set of ratios. Although by the standards of the first examples of the car the 1966 model was the least exciting in terms of equipment and specification, it was undeniably successful in competition, and relatively reliable both on and off the racetracks.

Whilst it could make the heart beat a little faster to even watch an example of this car, let alone actually drive one, they were something less than quick in making an exit from the dealers' showrooms. This was principally because the early cars were dogged with a poor record of reliability — for all of its handsome appearance, excellent power outputs and awesome noises, the

engine could be a real prima donna, slipping out of tune at the slightest excuse. Compound this with the way in which the rear axle could shake loose its bolts and deposit its oil all over the roadside, and the picture begins to come clear ...

By a strange series of twists and turns, it was this car which first gave us the RS dealerships, and subsequently the RS cars. When compared with the simple, quite fundamental, designs of the rest of the car range that Ford were selling at the time, the Lotus Cortina (Ford always sold it as a Cortina Lotus, but out of deference to the amount of work put into the car by Lotus, is is more commonly known as the Lotus Cortina) was so technically advanced and complicated that it scared the pants off a substantial number of dealerships. Consequently, the sales team at Ford came up with the RS concept — Sam Toy was the prime mover, aided and abetted by Walter Hayes and Terence Beckett — whereby a small number of dealers would undertake to train their workshop's leading lights in the care and maintenance of the twin-cammed Cortina. The dealers would also endeavour to offer a competitions unit, which would see a van in the paddock at race meetings in the area, and at local rallies. Even it if meant waiting at the end of a forest stage in the middle of Wales in the middle of a Saturday night, somebody would be there.

BJH 417 B

This particular car, now totally restored by owner Andy Middlehurst, was the actual car which won the British Saloon Car Championship, with the late, great, Jim Clark behind the wheel.

One of the pair of factory cars from 1964, the other bearing the plate BJH 418 B, this particular example is endowed with a slightly milder engine than that which was in place in 1964, but even so it still produces about 140 b.h.p. Ostensibly identical to the other Lotus Cortinas of the day, the car was actually slightly different in the suspension department, the major change being the addition of a rear anti-roll bar by Lotus.

Andy Middlehurst acquired the car almost three years ago, and subjected it to a total rebuild at the family workshops. Refinished in the original colours, the car is as clean underneath as it is from above. It has covered less than 11,000 miles from its date of registration in March 1964, and Andy has the full history of the car from the moment it first turned a wheel at the Lotus factory in Cheshunt.

The main differences between this and a road-going version of the car, besides the anti-roll bar, is the provision of a much larger fuel tank (with filler cap immediately behind the rear windscreen, rather than on the back panel of the car), and the replacement of the original front seats with a pair of vinyl-covered hip-hugging bucket seats. As it is a race machine there are no carpets to be seen throughout the interior, and, naturally, it has no spare tyre. Finally, the bonnet has a quick-release buckle to hold it down, and a matt-black flash across the leading edge.

Interestingly, there is no roll cage fitted to the car — this was the period when drivers wore Aertex short-sleeve sports shirts and, if they felt like, a cork crash helmet. By modern standards the spring rates of the car are very soft, and this led to a good deal of wheel-waving when the car was raced; it was nothing out of the ordinary to see one of these cars cornering on two wheels.

Andy Middlehurst, best-known as driver of a Golf GTi in ProdSaloons, has a fondness for his Lotus Cortinas — he has a second example at present undergoing a total rebuild — which is totally understandable; the car is still extremely rapid even by modern standards, and has that increasingly rare commodity of Character with a capital "C".

CORTINA LOTUS

◁ Being the way that they are, it took Ford but a little amount of time to instigate the idea and turn it into a reality, and even less time to realise what a potential goldmine they were sitting on. Nowadays, RS dealerships are coveted, but Ford have remained true to their original pledge, and ensure that no new RS dealership sets up in a territory already occupied by an existing dealership. The "network within a network" was an inspired piece of marketing strategy, and continues to provide Ford with a steady band of devoted customers — especially since they formalised everything with the RS 1600 back in the '60s.

"The Lotus Cortina was so advanced and complicated that it scared the pants off a substantial number of dealerships."

But back to the Lotus Cortina. In all, there were less than 2,900 of the machines ever built, and a good number of those have now disappeared from our roads forever — one tailslide too many? Of those, more than half were built with the leafspring rear axle, which means that the chances of picking up a coil-sprung specimen are rare indeed. Having said that, they do come up for sale from time to time, albeit at prices substantially in excess of the £1,100 which would have bought a new model back in 1963. Expect to pay about £9,000 for a pristine example — although less-than-perfect models can be bought for much less. The leaf-sprung (post June 1965) examples come cheaper, but again the differences between a perfect example and one which is in need of restoration can vary tremendously.

Surprisingly, spares are not altogether unobtainable — the owners club is the best source for these. Providing you are prepared to scout around, to pay out substantial sums of money for certain bits and pieces (mainly body panels and trim items), and prepared to take on a lot of work, it can be most worthwhile to buy a tatty example and rebuild it.

What you will get at the end of the day is a car which excites, which stimulates, which needs a lot of attention, which frustrates and delights. All in one — and if not in the same day, then almost certainly in the same week. In standard form the

engine still puts out as much power as a modern XR3i, but with something sorely lacking in the XR3i — that delightful wail as the cams really start to let the gases through, and the power out to the flywheel. And it is still possible to buy a tremendous range of tuning items for the engine, from wild cams to trick pistons, which will see the power approaching nearer to a hundred and fifty brake horsepower without sacrificing driveability. Yes, a well-sorted Lotus Cortina will see even a modern hot hatch, with its sophisticated suspension system and free-revving, economical, ecologically-sound engine, floundering to keep up ...

LOTUS CORTINA REGISTER

The scarcity of the Lotus Cortina has ensured that there is a healthy demand for an owners' club for the car, and this need is fulfilled by the Lotus Cortina Register. Both Mk I and Mk II examples of the car are catered for by the club, which keeps members in contact with each other by a variety of runs and events, as well as a lively and interesting magazine Quarter Bumper, which is produced four times each year.

A major function of the club is to supply information on keeping these cars mobile, not just by the availability of spares but also through the provision of advice and information.

The club can also be found displaying superb examples of the marque at shows up and down the country throughout the summer months.

For more information on the Lotus Cortina Register contact David Missions at Department P.F., Fern Leigh, Hornash Lane, Shadoxhurst, Ashford, Kent TN26 1HT.

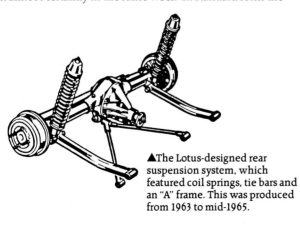

▲The Lotus-designed rear suspension system, which featured coil springs, tie bars and an "A" frame. This was produced from 1963 to mid-1965.

RS 1600

The first sixteen valve RS Escort

DENNIS FOY

Before I go any further, I have a confession to make; if there appears to be an unfair degree of bias towards the subject of this month's featured RS car, it is down to the fond memories that I hold of the RS 1600 that graced my driveway for a short time in the mid '70s.

If I close my eyes and sit quietly, it all comes back to me in a warm and rosy nostalgic glow. The raucous tones of the exhaust as I powered out of one bend and headed for the next. The scrabble of tyres as they fought for traction. The sharpness of the steering and the crispness of the gearchange. Ah yes, as Maurice Chevalier once sang, I remember it well.

When I bought the car it had been freshly rebuilt, and restored to street trim; like so many of its contemporaries, it had seen life as a rally car. It was painted in the then-trendy J.P.S. colours of gold pinstriping over a black base, and had a set of Minilite wheels. The cars weren't collectors' items then, and nobody really cared that much whether or not it was in the same trim and specification as it had been when it first emerged from Arisdale Avenue, South Ockendon — such attention to detail came later, as the collectability of the car became apparent. I owned the car for about a year, eventually selling it on because my heart had been won over by the siren song of a Lotus twin-cam living in an Elan roadster.

Those memories were rekindled recently, when Bob Quirk opened up his garage door to reveal his immaculate RS 1600. The car has been lovingly restored ("It was a bit of a wreck when I bought it ..."), and is finished in that favoured colour of FAVO cars, bright orange. The engine crackled into life immediately, and settled into that lumpy tickover that personifies the BDA engine. It took but a blip of the throttle to turn the burble into sheer music, and to send me wallowing into a mist of nostalgia.

The RS 1600 was the first production Ford to be fitted with a four-valves-per-cylinder engine. Cosworth were responsible for the head, which was a development of an earlier product of theirs, the FVA. The head used two camshafts, situated over the head, and these were driven by a toothed belt. The block was the Ford Crossflow Kent unit, and the original cam inside the block was left in place, to drive the oil pump and distributor. The engine was graced with a set of high-compression pistons (10:1) and came with either Dellorto or Weber sidedraught carburettors. The exhaust manifold was one of the best-designed ever to be found under the bonnet of a Ford, and the combination of these various components was enough to ensure that 120 b.h.p. at the flywheel was a reality. Because of the rules of racing and rallying at the time, which had a class break at 1600cc, the engine was homologated at 1601cc — which meant that it could be stretched by overboring to as much as two litres, whilst remaining class-legal. Leaving the engine block untouched and replacing the standard "mild" cams with something a little more radical was a common tweak of the day, and was enough to immediately put the power up by another twenty brake horsepower.

Behind the engine of the standard car was a four speed gearbox, the same as that found in all other sporting four-cylinder Fords of the day. It was also possible to order a ZF five-speed transmission as a standard factory fitment. At the rear of the car was a standard Sport axle (with 3.77:1 final drive ratio, though other gear sets could be specified), unless the customer had specified the ultra-tough Atlas axle when ordering the car.

Because of its intended usage as a competition machine, the basis of the car was a Type 49 version of the standard two-door Escort bodyshell. This was strategically stiffened along the main rails and around the bulkhead and suspension pickup points. The suspension system was basically MacPherson struts at the front with leaf springs at the rear, with the axle further located by a pair of tie bars from the half-shaft casing to the bodywork ▷

Besides the RS Owners' Club, full details of which were in last month's issue, there is another club to which owners of RS 1600s are attracted. This is the AVO Owners' Club, which is devoted to cars produced by Ford's Advanced Vehicle Operations at Halewood and at South Ockendon. The club has a lively social side, as well as an extensive competitions calendar throughout the season. They have amassed all manner of publications and literature concerning the cars which they cater for (the RS 1600, RS 2000 Mk I, RS 3100 Capri, Twin Cam Escort, and Escort Mexico), and these are available to members seeking guidance with running or rebuilding their cars. Each of the models is represented by a registrar, and then there is a Parts Secretary who is of great help to members looking for rare spares. A bi-monthly magazine (Havoc) keeps members aware of developments, as well as the individual opinions of members.

For full details of the club, contact the Membership Secretary, David Hibbin, at 53 Hallsfield Road, Bridgewood, Chatham, Kent ME5 9RS.

RS 1600

◁ on either side of the car. Early models of the car had the dampers of the rear suspension sitting at an angle of 65°, but from 1973 these were changed to almost upright positioning, as a result of development work carried out on the RS 2000. This resulted in later cars being less prone to oversteer than earlier models — a situation which virtually every rally driver immediately changed, by altering the rear spring and damper rates to restore the more-desirable oversteering characteristics.

The interior of the car was basically quite pleasant, a pair of semi-bucket seats up front, with a matching bench in the back. These could be had either in the standard perforated vinyl trim, or in one of several different types of cloth upholstery. Ahead of the driver was an RS steering wheel, behind which was situated a binnacle containing a large 140 m.p.h. speedometer, matching 8000 r.p.m. tachometer, and four smaller gauges which monitored temperature, oil pressure, fuel tank contents, and amperes. Loop-pile carpeting figured throughout, and it was possible to specify all manner of internal fitments, from a roll cage to a set of walnut cappings.

If you are starting to get a picture of this being a built-to-order car, then you are absolutely right; Ford sold the car under the banner of "The Potent Mix", and that was exactly what you got.

> "Ford sold the car under the banner of 'The Potent Mix' — and that is exactly what you got."

If you wanted your RS 1600 ready to go out and run in a rally, then it came from the factory like that. If, however, you had decided that your car was to be delivered in full road trim, with all of the luxury options, then it came through exactly the way that you had ordered it.

The list of options available to the fortunate few (less than 1,200 examples were ever built, the first few at Halewood but mostly at South Ockendon) was nothing short of stunning — the only things that you couldn't change were the very basic specifications of it having a Cosworth Twink head, a Type 49 bodyshell, and four wheels. Even the basic engine blocks differed; some cars were equipped with the basic Ford cast iron engine, whilst others had a Hart-produced alloy version. The latter offered no real benefits in standard form, but for competition use was ideal as it could be stretched right through to two litres safely (up to 120 b.h.p. per litre could be achieved with the alloy block), and had the added bonus of weighing less than the standard block.

Bob Quirk's car is about as close as you are likely to get to what is best described as a "textbook" example of the marque. It took over two years to restore the car, much of the time being taken up in locating parts, particularly trim items. The bodyshell was

stripped right down to bare metal, and repaired wherever replacement panels could not be found — even Bob's influence as head of the service department at Quicks of Manchester, one of the largest dealerships in the country, was not enough to ensure the availability of all of the many parts that were needed. The bodyshell was completely resprayed before the car was reassembled, and the engine was rebuilt. Bob's car has the alloy engine block, and this was one of the few aspects of the rebuild which posed no problem; fortunately there are still quite a few BDA engines in use in competition machines, and so components are still readily available from the likes of Burton Engineering.

The car has been finished inside to a very high specification, with abundant use of walnut veneer, a centre console, and black cloth trim — a vast improvement on the interior of my old example, which had the basic aluminium fascia trim, and vinyl seats.

Bob's daily drive is an RS Turbo Escort, and the two cars provide a fascinating set of contrasts; only ten brake horsepower separate the two cars, and their power-to-weight ratios are similar, as are their overall performance figures:-

	RS 1600	RS Turbo
b.h.p./ton	138	133
0-60 seconds	8.4	9.1
Maximum speed	115	124

The difference is in the way that they can be driven, and the way in which they achieve their figures. For instance, whilst the RS Turbo can be got into in a morning, and is as easy to drive when cold as it is once hot, the RS 1600 is downright anti-social until everything has thoroughly warmed through — for the first twenty minutes around town it is reluctant to rev freely, and the gearbox is given to resisting fast shifts. Running hard in the 1600 calls for great use of the gearshift to keep the revs above 4000, if the best is to be got from the engine. The RS Turbo, conversely, can be left in a gear much longer, as the turbo takes much of the

"The RS 1600 is downright anti-social until everything has warmed through."

need for dancing up and down the box away. The handling, too, is a world apart; the RS 1600 is given to hanging the tail out in the wet, whilst the Turbo's limited-slip viscous coupling takes much of the drama out of adverse weather driving. Finally, the braking system of the new car, with its SCS anti-lock system, is infinitely more sophisticated than that of the older car.

But all comparisons disappear out of the window when driving an RS 1600, as its character comes through. Somehow the driver forgives the car its little foibles as that lusty engine delivers the goods. The car is still precise in dry weather even by modern standards, and I can think of several hot hatchbacks that would be left floundering in the wake of a well-tuned RS 1600 in the hands of a capable driver.

The one thing that does tend to get forgotten in the rosy glow of nostalgia is quite how much work there is to be done, if the RS 1600 is to be kept in good running order. The carburettors shake about quite a bit, and are given to slipping out of tune at regular, frequent intervals. The bodywork of the early Escort, even in Type 49 specification, is prone to the rust-bug, and so regular underbody cleaning is essential. Finally, in view of the scarcity of trim pieces, it is essential to treat the interior gently.

Actually obtaining a good example of an RS 1600 is difficult, but not impossible. The various owners' clubs can be of assistance here, as owners tend to offer their cars for sale within the club first, before going "public" on the sale. When buying, check first that it is a genuine RS 1600 — the legend BATL L BFAT ... starting the sequence on the chassis identification plate. This confirms that the car is an RS 1600 produced at South Ockendon. Once you are satisfied that the car is a real 'un, it comes down to routine checks on the condition of the body and driveline. With the rest of the car at least acceptable, turn your attentions to the engine. This should be reasonably quiet, with no excessive noise from the valvetrain. These engines have always burnt a lot of oil (about a pint every 300 to 350 miles), so don't let a whiff of blue smoke as the car fires up put you off. If, however, there are great plumes of smoke coming from the back when the car is hot and running, beware; this could indicate bore wear, and this in turn could indicate a large bill for a rebore, and possibly a new set of pistons. Whatever you do, ensure that you give the car that you intend to buy a full road test, with the engine hot — only then will you be able to feel the benefits of (or spot the problems with) that superb engine and driveline.

The RS 1600, as Bob Quirk will attest, is not the easiest of cars to live with, primarily because of its need for attention, and the way that its character is transformed from beligerent when cold to benign when hot. But for all of its odd little ways, the car is an exciting machine to drive, and, in my opinion at least, the most desirable of the Mk I Escorts. And if that sounds biased, don't say I didn't warn you.   ●

ESCORT MEXICO

Built to celebrate Escort's finest hour

To describe the Mexico as a sheep in wolf's clothing could be construed as a little unkind, but it would not actually be that far from the truth. To the uninitiated, the car looked for all the world like an RS 1600, but a look under the bonnet would soon show that in place of the Cosworth-developed twin-cam engine was a relatively tame pushrod 1600. Yet for all of its mechanical simplicity — or perhaps because of it — the car fairly flew out of showrooms, and is to this day the single biggest-selling car to come from the RS stable, with a total of 10,300 examples built and sold.

The RS 1600 had set the ball rolling, attracting a new wave of interested customers to the otherwise-tame range of Escort saloons. However, many of those potential Rallye Sport customers were put off from actually ordering cars by the mechanical complexity of the twin-cam cars, which had already earned themselves a reputation as prima donnas. When Ford scored an overwhelming victory in the London-Mexico rally which preceded the World Cup in 1970, the wave of interest was phenomenal — but once again the salemen in RS dealerships found themselves faced with antipathy to the complex nature of the RS 1600.

The answer was to take the RS 1600, but instead of the twin-cam to install a far less complex 1600 GT Capri/Cortina engine. In all other respects the "new" car, which was to be named as the Mexico in honour of the World Cup Rally success, was the same as the RS 1600. This meant that it was based upon the strengthened "Type 49" version of the Escort two-door bodyshell, and was equipped with the 2000E four-speed gearbox as standard — although a less substantial clutch was installed, the heavy-duty item which backed up the twin-cam of the RS 1600 being deemed unnecessary. Heavy-duty suspension, an "English" axle, front disc brakes with servo-assistance, rear radius arms, and so forth completed the mechanical specification of the Mexico.

Externally, the car was identifiable by a fairly unsubtle set of stripes along each side of the car and across the bootlid, with the legend "Mexico" inset into the stripes as they crossed the doors of the car. Alternatively, the customer could specify what was known as a "delete option" (if you didn't specifically say that you didn't want the broad stripes you got them) and have the car delivered with far more discreet pinstripes and different badging; on each flank a metallic "Mexico" badge would feature, whereas the broad-striped car would bear the legend "1600 GT". The Mexico came standard with the same pressed steel wheels of the RS 1600, shod with 165 SR 13 radial tyres.

The inside of the car was more basic in its standard form than that of the RS 1600, with rubber mats in place of carpeting, less than adequate soundproofing, and seating shared with the "De Luxe", rather than the GT models of Escort. The car could,

ESCORT MEXICO

◁ however, be specified with a variety of optional extras, which would bring trim levels back up to those enjoyed by other RS owners. It was also possible to order such options as a roll cage, additional Cibie lighting, and so forth; basically anything that could be ordered for an RS 1600 (engine apart ...) could be specified for the Mexico.

The Mexico was nothing like as sharp in terms of acceleration and top speed as the RS 1600, but it was not too bad by the standards of the day; the 86 b.h.p. crossflow was able to propel the Mexico from 0-60 in about 10½ seconds, and the top speed was in the region of 100 m.p.h. When you took into account that the car cost substantially less than its more glamorous stablemate (£1,150 compared with £1,495), the loss in performance was made far more palatable.

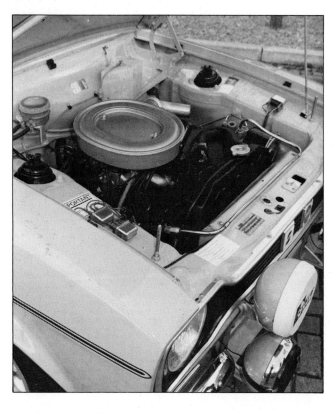

By RS standards, the Mexico remained relatively unchanged in its five year lifespan; the battery was relocated from the boot to under the bonnet in 1972, and at the same time the spare wheel was relocated in the side of the boot, rather than on the boot floor. Carpeting also became standard at this point, and the formal "Custom Pack" of improved trim items was also available for the car. In all other respects, the basic Mexico of 1975 was the same as the first cars which rolled off the line at South Ockendon in late 1970.

Having a package such as the Mexico gave the budget-conscious buyer a clear run at further development of the car. The driveline was designed to take 150 b.h.p. without the slightest complaint, and more could be put through it without making major changes. So versatile was the Kent crossflow engine that many owners started, usually the day that the warranty on the car ran

"THE MISTRESS"

This is the nickname given by Dave Hensley's wife to the bright yellow machine which features on these pages. Dave, Secretary of the Ford AVO Owners Club, has owned the car for more than a decade, and in that time it has, like so many other Mexicos, been heavily modified. At one point the engine was overbored, fitted with twin Weber DCOE carburettors, a wild cam and a Janspeed full-race exhaust system. The interior has been changed a couple of times, the suspension equipped with various different combinations of springs and dampers, and the exterior of the car tried with various combinations of striping kits.

However, as Dave himself put it, he "went all purist" a little while ago, and when the car finally reappeared on the road in February this year after a substantial rebuild it was as you see it now. The car features the "delete option" subtle striping, with Mexico badges on each front wing and on the bootlid. Those four spotlights are original equipment on the car, part of the Rallye Sport "clubman" package which also includes the alloy roll cage, the bucket seats, and a fireproof bulkhead. The Custom Pack also features on Dave's example of the Mexico, which is why the interior features such items as the real wood trim pieces and the centre console. In its lifetime the Hensley Mexico has worn wide steel wheels, and later RS four-spoke alloys. Now, however, it is equipped with RS-specification Minilite alloys and 185 x 13 tyres.

Under the bonnet, the visual effect is of a totally standard car, with a Weber 32/36 DGV carburettor, and original air cleaner case and exhaust manifold. However, the block itself is a shade larger than the standard 1600, with a total displacement of 1760cc – enough to provide ample power to blow away any XR3i which has the temerity to try and take on Dave. I've seen it happen ...

To ensure that the handling is as good as it ought to be with that sort of power on tap, Dave has stiffened the rear spring rates, and fitted a set of gas-controlled dampers on all four corners of the car. The original braking system has proved itself more than capable of dealing with its required duties.

Dave uses the car virtually as a daily driver, and still gets as much fun from running the car as he ever has – and how many drivers can honestly claim that ten years on?

out, to replace various standard components with pieces which would develop more power. For instance, taking off the standard carburettor and replacing it with a pair of Dellorto or Weber sidedraughts would immediately put the power output up to about 100 b.h.p. A change of camshaft could easily add a further twenty horses, and a change of cylinder head to one with improved porting and bigger valves could add yet more power to the flywheel output figure. In short, it was easy to get the Mexico's engine to develop more power than the 110 b.h.p. that the RS 1600's unit would develop in standard form.

A vast range of aftermarket pieces exists for the crossflow engine, up to and including oversized forged pistons which would suit an overboring of the block. These could also be ordered with a revised dome which would raise the compression ratio beyond the standard 9:1. A much-favoured package sees the engine displacing 1760cc, fitted with 10:1 pistons and revised cam-train, big-valve head and twin carburettors – and a total power output in the region of 150 b.h.p. for street use. For competition use, it is possible to build an example of this engine which makes closer to 200 b.h.p. – although regular rebuilds are the rule with engines in that state of tune.

And it wasn't just the engine which could be uprated: dozens of different spring combinations were available (and still are

such devices as the Renault 5 and the Fiesta XR2 challenges, with full grids of essentially identical cars being driven hard by drivers of varying degrees of skill.

If you have been given the impression that the standard Mexico was a bit boring, then I apologise for misleading you; in standard form they were fun to drive – when modified effectively, they become downright exciting transport.

The standard Mexico handled well, sharing its suspension settings and damper rates, as well as its steering geometry, with the RS 1600. A natural neutral attitude was the order of the day, although in the wet they could display a tendency to hanging out the tail. Whilst there was nothing like as much power on tap as there would be with a twink under the bonnet, there was still enough to allow the car to make quite rapid progress – especially if good use is made of the gearbox. Fortunately, the combination of a light clutch and that oh-so-slick gearshift made changing gear a pleasurable experience.

obtainable from a variety of sources), and there are a number of very good damper packages to be had for this car which take the already-good handling to even greater levels. Various manufacturers offer other items essential to the successful uprating of a car, like fast-ratio steering racks, uprated braking systems (from high performance pads through to complete new sets of discs and calipers) and so forth.

It therefore figures that the chances of obtaining a completely standard Mexico, one which is exactly as it was when it first rolled out of Ford AVO, are slim indeed. The Mexico sold to enthusiasts, and most enthusiasts couldn't help but exploit the massive amount of potential that the Mexico offered. The cars were intended by Ford to be road cars, but many examples have at some point been rallied or raced – in fact in the early '70s Shell Oils sponsored the ShellSport Mexico challenge, a series of pro-am races at Brands Hatch. This was the beginning of the One Marque race series which still continue to this day with

The Mexico was, in fact, a very "user friendly" sort of car, having a chassis which was designed for far more power than the engine could provide in standard form – it proved extremely difficult to lose one of these cars in the dry, such were its inherent good manners. With a mildly-tuned engine producing, say, 110 or 115 b.h.p., it became far more demanding to drive, but rewarded the driver with an adrenalin burn that few cars at the price could even approach.

In view of the scarcity of original-specification cars, the chances are that the potential buyer will end up with a car which has been modified in some manner or other. This, generally speaking, is probably no bad thing – provided that the modifications have been effectively and safely carried out. The things to look out for are neat and tidy installations, with no oddball wiring/fixing/clamping and the like. Items like twin carburettors ought really to be installed using a well-made, and purpose-designed, throttle linkage, and with all fuel pipe ▷

ESCORT MEXICO

connections properly seated and clamped – the basic rule is to beware of the bodge-up, as a good worker is a tidy worker – and the person who expects a car which is obviously lashed together with tape and a prayer to run properly is fooling nobody but themselves.

As regards the matter of what is and is not a fair price to pay for a Mexico, this is very much one of those "piece of string" issues. I have seen outwardly similar examples of the car on offer for wildly different prices, and the only advice that I can offer to a prospective buyer is to seek out a good example of the beast, and then be prepared to haggle, until you reach a price which is agreeable to both yourself and the vendor.

The issue of keeping one of these cars mobile is equally complex. Ford still have quite a few of the main body panels available, and where they do not, pattern panels and repair pieces are available through good motor factors. However, having said that, pieces such as inner wings and bulkhead panels are no longer available for the Type 49 bodyshell. Fortunately, the Ford AVO Owners Club are working hard on this problem, and avidly looking into wither the supply of alternative parts or modifying standard parts available for the normal Mk I Escort range.

The mechanical components of the car are no problem whatsoever. In addition to many components being still available from Ford dealerships, just about every speed shop worth its salt (KDM is a good example) stock enough bits to either restore a standard model, or modify one to the owners' content.

The only really difficult part of keeping a Mexico on the road is in the provision of trim panels. These, like those of most early RS cars, vary from scarce to unobtainable – of particularly difficulty are such items as the rear parcel shelf, and the rear quarter trim panels from either side of the seat. Withers of Winsford are probably the best place to start looking for these rarer panels if your local dealership confirms their unavailability. And once again, the Ford AVO Owners Club are seriously looking into the supply of new items modelled exactly on the original pieces.

Whatever the trials and tribulations of obtaining and running a Mexico may be, the basic fact remains that it is most worthwhile: the car is not only rewarding in its own right as a driving machine, but it is also turning out to be a most worthwhile investment, with particularly good examples selling at premium rates. ●

RS CAPRIS

Sports hatches gain their RS credentials

DENNIS FOY

R ight from the outset, the Capri was a natural choice to receive the Rallye Sport treatment. It was, after all, "the car you've always promised yourself", the most overtly sporting Ford ever seen in production on this side of the Atlantic Ocean.

It was 1970 when the first Capri to bear the RS tag appeared. This was a development of the German Capri 2600 GT, and came about as the result of calls from Ford's Competition Manager in Germany, Jochen Neerpasch, to produce a lightweight version of the production car for competition use. Between then and 1974 there were to be something like 4,000 of these cars built, but there were tremendous variations to be found in them, depending upon their intended use. Typical of this is the way in which the first batch of cars, which went straight to Herr Neerpasch's department, were fitted with lightweight glassfibre bonnet, bootlid, and door panels, whereas production variants wore the same steel panels as their lesser sisters, the 2600 GTs.

The German V6 Capris utilised the Cologne engine, the same basic block as that still in use today powering the XR4x4 and Granada 2.9 models. The size ▷

RS CAPRIS

◁ of the engine in the 2600 GT was 2520cc, but for the RS version a longer throw crank was inserted which brought up the displacement to a more realistic 2637cc. High compression pistons were also added to the car, which took the ratio up to 10.5:1. But the main difference between the engine of the RS 2600 and its little sister the 2600 GT was that the RS came with fuel injection.

This was a mechanical system, designed by Weslake Engineering of Rye but based upon the German Kugelfischer mechanical system, rather than the Bosch electronic injection which would be used on a modern car. Looking back, the system seems positively antiquated, but after a few teething troubles were sorted out it ran well, and provided enough fuel to enable the engine to produce about 150 b.h.p. Driven by a crankshaft belt and controlled by a tri-pointed camshaft which read engine speed, throttle opening and manifold vacuum, the mechanical system was to prove reliable throughout the life of the car.

One disadvantage of the engine choice was that the Cologne V6 uses siamesed port cylinder heads — it has only two ports to each bank of three cylinders, which means that there was ultimately a strangling effect of exhaust gases. For racing, Weslake developed six-port heads, which were far more satisfactory, but these were never fitted to the factory production cars.

In terms of power, the 150 b.h.p. that was produced by the engine was quite adequate, and to ensure that it got through to the ground properly, a few changes were made from the 2600 GT's mechanical specification. The gearbox was replaced with a close-ratio item from a Taunus, the brakes were uprated by the use of an eight inch servo to feed the otherwise-standard disc and drum set-up, and a final drive ratio of 3.2:1.

The main changes to the underpinnings of the car were the substitution of competition standard suspension components, including what some have described as over-stiff front coil springs.

Rear single leaf springs and an anti-roll bar located the rear axle, and RS-specification bushings were used throughout the suspension system. Bilstein dampers were used on each corner. A fast-response steering rack was used, and the front wing wheelarches were flared to allow adequate clearance for the wide Minilite wheels when on full lock.

Externally the car was identifiable by its abundant stickers, and by its lack of such items as full-width bumpers — the car's racing lineage was clearly carried over to the production run.

In terms of performance, the road car was shiny and sharp, if not exactly earth-shattering by modern standards. 0-60 took about eight seconds, and the car's top speed was in the order of 125 m.p.h. However, it wasn't so much what the car did on paper, as what it could manage on the road. The mid-range punch was exceptionally good, and the car's handling was crisp and racecar responsive — every inch of the car

THE RALLYE SPORT SERIES HOW AND WHY

THE RALLYE SPORT SERIES HOW AND WHY

Ford's first serious road-and-track car was the Lotus Cortina, which first arrived on the scene in 1963. Taking an example of Ford's latest mid-sized "peoples' car" and powering it with a sophisticated twin-cam engine, backed up by an equally sophisticated chassis, was popular with everybody but about half of the Ford dealer network.

To overcome resistance to the car, Sam Toy and the Board at Ford of Britain hatched a plan to develop the Rally Sport (the "E" on Rallye came later) network-within-a-network.

Dealers were canvassed, and about seventy of them agreed to not only train their staff to deal with the Lotus Cortina (Ford let it be known that other, similarly sports-orientated cars were also in the pipeline, as a means of holding their interest in the programme), but also to make staff available at racetracks, clubman rallies, and so forth throughout the weekends.
Ford have never looked back since, and the RS network has since grown to almost twice the size.
There is now a "waiting list" of dealerships after an RS franchise.

The first car to appear with the RS badge on it was the RS 1600 Escort, in 1970. Since that time there have been RS versions of the Escort and Capri, and most recently, the Sierra.
The RS marque is viewed now as it was then by Ford — the tag is reserved for the serious enthusiasts' cars, for those who race or rally — or aspire to.
Then comes the XR series — no competition intention here, just good fast road cars — and at the bottom of the tree are the L, GL, and so forth.

By adopting such a "snobbish" attitude to the RS marque, the currency has never been debased, and it is still the marque of a serious motor car.
Such branding has been tried by other manufacturers, but nobody has ever succeeded like Ford have.

▲The original RS 2600 used the Cologne V6 engine. 4,000 were built between 1970 and 1974.

tingled, and the driver was constantly aware of what the four corners of the car were doing — or wanted to do. Roadholding was exceedingly good, and the RS 2600 was, in summary, an exciting and stimulating car to drive.

During its lifetime, the RS 2600 achieved considerable success on the racetracks of Europe, in the hands of such legends as Jochen Mass, Hans Stuck and Ronnie Petersen. Engine sizes of the racers varied between 2.6 and 2.9 litres, depending upon class requirements, and the specification of the racers bore little resemblance to what Herr Schmidt could buy from his local Ford Werke dealership. The final production models rolled off the line at Saarlouis in 1974.

By about halfway through the RS 2600 programme, Ford Germany had lost a chunk of their interest in the Capri programme, favouring instead the Escorts which were winning races and rallies with startling regularity. Plans were already being laid for another RS Capri, this time here in England.

This was the RS 3100, which utilised the chassis of the German car, but used as a power source a modified version of the 3.0 Essex V6 engine. The road version of the car was somewhat short of radical in any area, and the engine typified the safe approach that was adopted; whilst Ford were aware that the engine could be overbored to a little over 3220cc, and could be fitted with a long-throw crankshaft which would give more than 3.6 litres, they opted to stick with a mild overbore to 95.19mm (the standard engine had a bore of 93.7mm) which gave a displacement of 3091cc. The heads were mildly polished and ported and the manifolds were matched accordingly, but in all other respects the engine was the same as that of the 3.0 Capri. The modifications were still, for all of their conservative nature, adequate to gain 10 b.h.p. over the standard engine's 138 brake horsepower, even if it relied on a single 2-choke carburettor for its fuel feed.

Backing up the engine was the familiar four-speed transmission which was to be found in all 3000 Capris of the day, and a standard-pattern rear axle, but with a 3.09:1 final drive ratio. Suspension and brakes were to the same specification as the RS 2600, although slightly softer damping could be specified as a no-cost option.

The main difference from the outside of the car was the adoption of a bootlid spoiler — an item which ought to have been homologated onto the original RS Capri, but had not been, much to the chagrin of the German race teams, who were experiencing rear stability problems at very high speeds. As with the earlier RS Capri, the 3.1 had quarter bumpers and a spoiler at the front, and all trim items on the outside of the shell were finished in very trendy matt black.

The additional torque of the 3.1 engine was enough to knock anything up to a half-second off the 0-60 time when compared with the German car, and mid-range acceleration was equally improved. The additional weight of the Essex engine altered the handling characteristics, with the RS 3100 having a penchant for pronounced understeer when pushed hard in the dry. In the wet it was like any other V-engined Capri — tail happy.

The chassis, being virtually identical to that of the RS 2600, was lively and informative to the driver, and the greater precision of the British-specification gearbox contributed to make the RS 3100 even more of a driver's car. Body roll was virtually non-existent, and the car could be pressed through a series of bends at far higher speeds than could ever be attempted in a standard 3.0 Capri. It is no surprise that these cars are now much sought-after collectors' items.

Altogether there were something like a couple of hundred RS 3100 Capris built at Halewood, but due to delays in getting

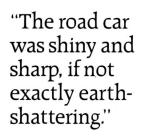

"The road car was shiny and sharp, if not exactly earth-shattering."

the car homologated for racing, the Mk II Capri was already in production before the RS cars were offered for sale. Because of this, and because the oil crisis was biting deep, Ford experienced some difficulty in selling the machines, and much discounting went on. That was the end of the RS Capri as an official production car. ▷

RS Capris enjoyed much racing success in Europe, particularly with Mass, Stuck, and Petersen behind the wheel. ▼

RS CAPRIS

The RS 3100 was intended to have been homologated with a build of a thousand units, in order to qualify the car for racing, but then, as still happens today, less-than-thorough checking by the authorities meant that the projected figure was never reached. Even so, the RS 3100 found its way onto circuits across Europe, and it achieved a fair degree of success; Ralf Stommelen won several times in one at Nurburgring, Karl Ludwig did likewise at Hockenheim, and Jochen Mass beat the opposition at the Norisring in an RS 3100 in 1975. The car's last official appearance on a track was in November 1985 at Kyalami, South Africa, when it failed to finish due to engine failure.

Yet whilst the RS Capri officially ceased to exist when production ended in 1974, there were still cars being produced which were entitled to wear the RS badge as late as 1980. The reason for this is the simplicity of the original RS 3100 concept, combined with the amenability of the RS facility.

lowered, stiffened front coil springs and the single leaf, uprated rear springs. RS bushes were installed throughout, and the anti-roll bars from the original RS programme were fitted. However, in place of the original specification Bilstein dampers, this particular car, just like the 16 others which were similarly modified over a several-year period, was fitted with Koni adjustable units which offer a more precise degree of control.

Under the bonnet, RS continued their tradition by painting the rocker covers of the engine in Ford blue, just as every RS Capri had always been. On the outside of the car the white paintwork was augmented by a set of diagonal stripes in RS colours on each side, and a smaller flash on the tailgate. Finally, authentic RS decals were applied to the sides and back of the car, together with the legend "Prepared by Ford Rallye Sport".

Whether or not purists would agree that this is a true RS is debatable, but what is beyond dispute is that the car, now

▲The RS 3100 was built at Halewood, using the Capri 2000 as a base. About 200 were produced in 1974.

one either — a couple of tenths of a second on the sprint to sixty and a couple of miles per hour on the top speed are about all that are in it.

Finding examples of genuine RS Capris is about as easy as striking gold in the foothills of the Welsh mountains — not impossible, but far from simple. One or two examples of the original German car found their way to our shores, notably a pair which were specially built with right-hand-drive controls for a couple of Ford senior executives. The occasional left-hander crops up from time to time, but almost without exception these have seen better days, and are in need of full restoration — either that, or somebody has already carried out the work, and is asking a proportionally outrageous price for the car.

Of the RS 3100, examples of this do crop up occasionally, but invariably these are offered for sale by a knowledgeable owner who is fully aware of the scarcity of the car — and again, prices are on the high side. Unlike certain other RS cars (the main one being the RS 2000) there seem to be few imposters around — those of which I have become aware have been so badly bodged together that identifying them from the real thing took only seconds. If you do manage to get hold of an example of a real RS Capri you will have a very satisfying car on your hands, once the mechanical specification has been restored to good order — pay particular heed to the suspension bushings and to the dampers, as excess wear in these components can so easily render the car awful to drive.

The car which features most prominently on these pages is typical of the genre, starting life originally as a 3000S Mk III. This car ran for the first 25,000 miles of its life in original form, but was then taken in to Boreham and converted to full RS 3100 specification. The engine was removed, rebuilt, and overbored to the required 95.19mm — which gave it the entitlement to be called a 3100. The suspension was removed, and replaced with the

owned by policeman Rod Carter from Cheadle Hulme in Cheshire, is right. It looks right, with its contrasting stripes, low stance and Minilite wheels and low-profile tyres, and it makes real RS 3100 noises from the open end of its twin tailpipes. It handles better than any normal Capri 3.0S, and the extra ten or so horsepower endow the car with tighter and sharper response through the gears. Its performance is not quite up to that of a 2.8i Capri, but it isn't that far behind

Finally, if you do buy yourself an RS Capri, ensure that your insurance cover is realistic, and that you will be able to claim a full and genuine open-market value should the worst happen, and the car be either stolen or written off. And do what Rod Carter has done, and add a set of high-security locks to protect your investment. ●

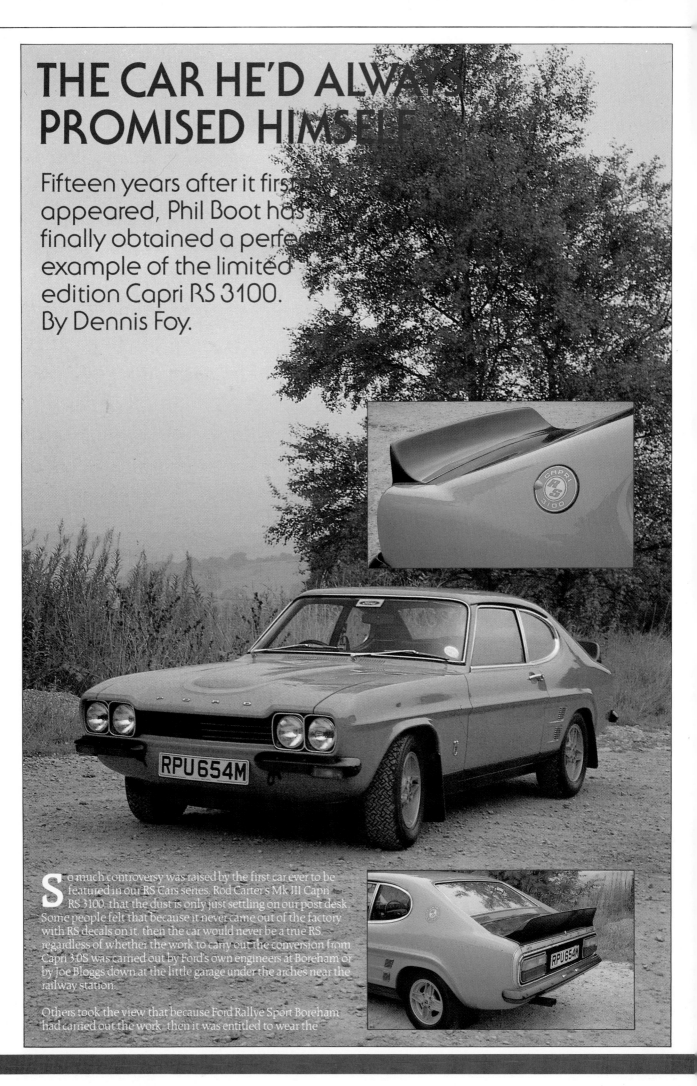

THE CAR HE'D ALWAYS PROMISED HIMSELF...

Fifteen years after it first appeared, Phil Boot has finally obtained a perfect example of the limited edition Capri RS 3100. By Dennis Foy.

So much controversy was raised by the first car ever to be featured in our RS Cars series, Rod Carter's Mk III Capri RS 3100, that the dust is only just settling on our post desk. Some people felt that because it never came out of the factory with RS decals on it, then the car would never be a true RS, regardless of whether the work to carry out the conversion from Capri 3.0S was carried out by Ford's own engineers at Boreham or by Joe Bloggs down at the little garage under the arches near the railway station.

Others took the view that because Ford Rallye Sport Boreham had carried out the work, then it was entitled to wear the coveted RS nomenclature. But whatever the arguments, there was a common thread — virtually everybody said that they would like to see something on the original Mk I RS 3100. Therefore, when Philip Boot of Derbyshire contacted us to say that his restoration project was finally completed (we were already aware of his ownership of the car), it was the perfect opportunity to get together a full story on the Halewood-built Capri RS.

Phil's interest in owning an example of the car can be traced back to the time when the cars were freshly on sale. His best friend called around to see him one day in a Modena green Capri — a bespoilered, wide-wheeled, keylined beauty of an RS 3100. The car was the state of the art in Capris, and Phil coveted it.

Time came and went, and Phil's commitments to marriage, home and job precluded his ownership of an RS Capri. Whilst his friend let his RS 3100 pass into fresh ownership and Phil himself put thoughts of ever owning one to the back of his mind, the aspiration to have an RS 3100 of his own one day never really left him.

A little under a year ago, family Boot were driving through the outskirts of Manchester when Phil spotted a rather sad-looking green Capri sitting in the car park of a pub — it was a Modena

had her husband committed to the nearest asylum. However, she was fully aware of what the car meant to Phil, and was equally in favour of its restoration. An additional stroke of luck was that the previous owner was also aware that the car she had owned was an RS, and had always gone to great pains during her seven years of ownership to ensure that only RS parts were fitted to the car, and that nothing vital had been lost.

Yet for all the car's authenticity, it was in quite a state. The bodywork was doing a pretty good impression of a colander, most of the trim pieces on the outside were in an advanced state of disintegration, and the interior was nothing short of a mess. It was shaping up to be a major project.

Work started almost immediately, but not on the car itself; the first move was to spend time locating the many components which were needed, and the second was to do some work on the garage — widening it, fitting it out, and adding a storage heater to overcome the coldness of the approaching winter. Parts came from a variety of sources, principally KT Group in Kent (Ford RS main dealers who are experts at locating authentic pieces for RS cars, thanks to the knowledge of Jeff Mann of their counter staff), and from New Ford Parts Centre in Chorley, Lancashire. Many of the smaller trim items came Phil's way by another excellent stroke of luck; purely by chance he was

No Capri RS 3100 ever came off the Halewood production line in such good condition — all credit to this must go to Phil Boot.

green RS 3100 which might have seen better days — but was still businesslike enough to rekindle the flame. Phil took a note of the car's registration details, which looked more than a little familiar, and asked his friend if that was the same car which he had once owned. It wasn't — but only two digits on the registration number separated the cars.

What followed was a neat series of twists which eventually led to the owner of the car which had been spotted. Phil's company had an office not far from the pub at which the Capri had been spotted, and he rang the switchboard operator there to see if she could discover the telephone number of the pub — only to find that another member of staff at the office worked there on a part-time basis and happened to know that the owner of the Capri was a barmaid at the pub — and that yes, she did want to sell the car. Eventually Phil arrived on the doorstep of the car's owner and offered to buy the Capri, which by this point had been taken off the road as it had run out of test certificate, and needed some work before it could get a fresh one. Ten minutes later, Phil Boot was about £300 lighter in his wallet — but he did own a genuine RS Capri, one of only two hundred ever built. Phil is fortunate indeed to have a wife who is understanding, because when he first brought home the latest addition to the stable, anybody would have been sympathetic had Mrs. Boot

offered an absolutely immaculate Mk I Capri 1.6GT for a very reasonable sum. He bought the car, raided it for all of the necessary items (replacing them with less-good parts from a number of sources), and then sold the car on again at a slight profit!

Much of the credit for the present condition of the Capri's bodywork must go to RS Autos of Furness Vale in Derbyshire, who have done an excellent job of affixing all of the new panels which have been fitted to the bodyshell and repairing those areas for which replacements were unavailable. The rebuild process followed the usual sequence, with all mechanical parts being removed from the bodyshell, along with the entire contents of the interior of the car and all of the glass and external trim. It is that part of the process which can cause the soul-searching — only then is the magnitude of a rebuild project really apparent, and it is at that stage that so many people decide to abandon the whole idea and get rid of the mountain of bits and pieces that go into a car.

Being aware of this potential minefield, Phil Boot took the precaution of buying as much of the required selection of new items as possible. That way, when the project hit that crisis point he felt that he had already committed so much time, effort and ▶

cold hard cash to the cause that it would be sheer folly not to continue with the rebuild.

What remained of the original bodyshell after all of the diseased panelwork had been amputated was shotblasted to remove every last trace of rust, and the car was immediately primed. The new panels and repairs were then added and effected by Chris at RS Autos, all of the work being to an extraordinarily high standard. Much of the repair work is hidden away from view now that the car is complete and running, which is something of a pity; having seen a sequence of photographs taken at the time of the body rebuild I can honestly say that the amount of effort, skill and ingenuity that went into creating such items as floorpan inserts, rear wheelarch liners, and inner front wing edges is nothing short of phenomenal.

manufacturer. However, by dint of diligence, ingenuity and sheer hard work Phil has managed to pull together everything necessary to restore the inside of his car to as-new condition. It has taken nine months to get the car into the shape it is in today, along with an amount of money which would go a long way towards buying a new XR2. In fact, to raise the necessary finance to get the project underway, the Boots sold their family XR2 and replaced it with a far more basic model of Fiesta. They are both understandably immensely proud of their RS 3100, and so they ought to be — it is without doubt the best example of the model to be seen on British roads.

Yet not everybody agrees. Within days of getting the car finished, and a week before these photographs were taken, they decided to take the car down to the RS Owners Club national day in

Interior of the Capri features bucket seats in black vinyl. Tatty originals were totally restored by Philip Boot.

Once the repairs had been carried out, and the new front wings, screen scuttle, doors and so forth had been fitted to the shell, Chris's partner Simon took over, and resprayed the entire bodyshell inside and out with fresh Modena green paint. The result of all of the effort that went into the car at RS Autos (including Phil Boot's — he acted as general labourer as a means of keeping the final bill down to a tolerable level), is a bodyshell which is substantially better than that of any Capri which came off the production line at Halewood.

When he wasn't at the bodyshop, Phil was keeping himself occupied working on the small mountain of components which were piled up in his garage. The previous owner had told Phil that the engine was rebuilt a couple of years ago, but just to be certain he stripped and reconditioned it. The original engine which came within the engine bay from new, it runs sweetly and cleanly. The rest of the mechanical componentry tells a similar tale, with everything being checked over, thoroughly cleaned up, and reconditioned as necessary.

The first part of a car to show signs of wear and tear is the interior, and paradoxically it is trim parts which are always the first section to be struck from the availability list by the car's

Leicestershire. Even before their wheels had stopped rolling they overheard somebody saying that he "would bounce the car from the concours competition if it was up to me ... After all, those decals are wrong, and the wheels aren't right either". Fortunately, it was not up to that person, and the Capri went on to win a major award.

The parts to which the expert referred were appended and amended respectively by Phil, who felt them to be appropriate to his particular car. The side decals are based closely on those which were affixed to the RS 2600, the first RS Capri, and I

> "For all the car's authenticity, it was in quite a state when it was first acquired."

Huge, deformable rear spoiler was unique to RS 3100. Few of the factory examples fitted onto the bootlid quite as tidily as this one does!

judging with a known authority — and discovered that to be absolutely perfect for that class of judging it ought to have not only all of the trim items, decals and so forth exactly as they were on the original production run of cars, but also such details as overspray beneath the car from where the sills had been sprayed black, underbonnet stickers ought not be affixed perfectly square and true and so on and so forth — the principle is that the production line workers wouuld have done that, so a restorer ought to do likewise. Personally, I would take the same attitude as Phil Boot, and build the car up as close to perfectly as is possible.

Phil was good enough to offer me the opportunity to try the car out for myself when we took it out to photograph it, and the first thing that struck me was that from the moment that I turned the key and the 3091cc V6 engine burst into gruff, burbling life, I was totally aware that I was behind the wheel of an RS car — there was that special "tingling" sensation coming through all of the controls that is peculiar to Rallye Sport models from the Ford stable, which makes them such a pleasure to drive. The steering of the car is pleasantly weighted, neither too heavy nor too light, and the driver is constantly aware of what the big Pirelli CN36 tyres are doing.

The other controls are similarly weighted and balanced, with such details as equal pedal height and spacing having been

The 3091cc Essex V6 produces 148 b.h.p. — enough to give excellent performance even by today's standards.

concur with Phil entirely — they suit the car perfectly, and tell the world what the green car is in a manner already adopted by Ford of Germany. And the wheels? Technically, they ought to have polished rims. However, the original alloys were severely pitted and would not polish up, and so Phil opted to have them refinished in a soft grey — and again, they suit the car perfectly.

Out of curiosity, Phil discussed the whole concept of concours

CONTACTS

KT Ford Group, The Brent, Dartford, Kent.
Telephone: 0322 22171.

New Ford Parts Centre, Abbey Mill, Abbey, Chorley, Lancs
Telephone: 0254 830343.

RS Autos, Furness Vale Industrial Estate, Furness Vale, Derbys
Telephone: 0663 45665.

attended to at the design stage. The gearchange action is positive without being baulky, and the overall impression is of a car that is surprisingly easy to drive smoothly. Body roll and ride quality are excellently controlled (Phil took the precaution of fitting new Bilstein dampers at each corner of the car), and braking action is smooth, progressive, and, most importantly, effective, thanks to the big ventilated discs with which the front hubs are blessed. I would have welcomed the chance to spend a few hours behind the wheel, exploring the car's abilities much further — but then, who wouldn't?

At the end of nine months' hard work, resourcefulness, cash, and everything else that has gone into the car, Phil Boot has finally achieved more than he had hoped for back in 1973 — he at last has his Capri RS 3100, and it is better than any factory example could have been. And what is particularly pleasing to discover is that he doesn't intend to have it as a no-go show car; quite the contrary. This car is going to be driven, and driven as hard or as easily as the mood and conditions dictate. It is insured for use all of the year round, and so if the fancy takes them to go out and put some miles on their Modena green machine, the Boots will do so. And if my brief experience behind the wheel is anything to go by, it will be enjoyment all the way. ●

RS 2000

The most popular RS Escorts ever

DENNIS FOY

It was Ford of Germany who were responsible for the original concept of the RS 2000 as a production vehicle. Already impressed by customer reaction to the Escort Mexico and its rarer stablemate the RS 1600, the Germans were astute enough to realise that there was room for a third model. What they were looking for was a car which had performance levels approaching those of the RS 1600, but without the mechanical complexity of that car. They were also after a car with a more comfortable and comprehensive interior specification — but they wanted all of this for a price which was somewhere between those of the RS and the Mexico. The design brief was handed to Ford's Advanced Vehicle Operation at South Ockendon in Essex, and the Germans awaited their reply.

purely physical one of slotting the engine, which had originally been designed for the American Pinto compact range, into the confines of the Escort's engine bay. Move one was to design a completely new sump for the engine, which would clear the front "axle" crossmember. The new part was cast in aluminium, and contained baffles which would prevent oil surge problems. The gearbox too caused problems, being totally different from any previously seen in an Escort; legend has it that production workers at South Ockendon (which is also known as Aveley) found it necessary to resort to the use of a lump hammer in the area of the transmission tunnel, in order to gain adequate clearance. A new bellhousing was cast in aluminium to reduce weight, and to better suit the Escort's bodyshell. To keep the split of weight front-to-rear similar to that of the RS 1600, there was no room for the engine-driven fan of the Pinto unit, and so an electric fan was installed, just ahead of the radiator. This last move brought with it a bonus, as it freed another two brake horsepower from the engine — which gave the RS 2000 a tidy 100 b.h.p. power output.

To deal with the differences in weight between this engine and others used in the Sporting Escorts, it was necessary to alter the suspension settings; when compared with the RS 1600, the two-litre model's front suspension was some 30% uprated, whilst at the rear it was softened by about 7% via a reduction in the damper ratings. The complete car sat an inch closer to the ground than a Mexico. ▷

F.A.V.O., in typical fashion, delivered the goods. Using the same reinforced bodyshell as the other sporting Escorts, the RS 2000 employed under its bonnet the single overhead camshaft two litre engine that was to be found in the Cortina 2.0 GT, complete with matching four speed transmission. The level of trim and equipment was a substantial improvement on that found in the RS 1600 and the Mexico. Most important of all, the cost of the car fell just about halfway between those of the other two Escort variants which had encouraged its creation — the Mexico at the time cost £1,274, the RS 2000 £1,442, and the RS 1600 of the day cost in the order of £1,760.

The first problem that Ford A.V.O. had to overcome was the

RS 2000

◁ On the inside of the car the difference between this Escort and the other two mentioned was immediately apparent. Superbly designed cloth-covered bucket seats were a standard fitment, and the car's floor was covered with a high-grade carpet. A flat, three-spoked thick-rimmed steering wheel was also standard, and the car came with the six-clock instrument cluster common to the sportier models of Escort. Beyond the standard trim there were options such as wooden fascia cappings and a centre console with radio available, and many of the surviving examples of RS 2000 have these — which indicated that most customers specified them from new.

External identification of the RS 2000 was simple for anybody with even partial sight; in addition to the 5½" wide four-spoke Ford alloy wheels, and the suitably flared wheelarch lips, the cars came standard with a set of less-than-subtle stripes, eight inches high along the length of each side, with corresponding (but smaller) stripes on the bonnet and the bootlid. Black and chrome RS 2000 badges completed the identity process.

As was common with all Fords of the day, and particularly with the RS models, the basic delivery price of the car was supplanted with a list of options — the alloy wheels were optional extras, in fact — and one of those appears on the example in our photographs, in the form of the front chin spoiler. This particular car is a concours-winning model belonging to Paul Corkhill from Blackpool, and it is extremely well-restored, as our photographs (hopefully) show. Totally faithful to the original specification, the orange car features yellow stripes, and the interior is in black, with the optional radio and console package, and wood veneer trim strips. Buying the car new with those items would have added something like £80 to the cost of the car at its launch, with another £100 or thereabouts for the wheels and spoiler.

To drive, the car was as close to being all things to all men as Ford have ever achieved with an RS car; it was docile and predictable in traffic, the engine producing adequate torque even at quite low engine speeds, and the ride being quite acceptably smooth over all but the roughest of road surfaces. Yet when the conditions allowed the throttle could be floored, and the engine would urge the car forward smoothly and rapidly. The gearshift was as clean as a knife through butter, and the ratios were spaced almost perfectly for fast runs along winding roads. The final drive ratio was quite high (3.54:1, when most ordinary Escorts had a differential ratio of 4.1:1) and this, together with abundant soundproofing, contributed greatly to the overall civilised nature of the car — motorway cruising at 70 m.p.h. in top gear would have the engine running at a mere 3600 r.p.m., an economical and unfussy speed. Pushed to its limit the Mk I RS 2000 could achieve a maximum speed of 109 m.p.h., and would make the sprint to sixty in nine seconds, give or take a tenth — contemporary road tests have got the time down to as little as 8.8 seconds, but others went as "slowly" as 9.3 seconds. So nine seconds is about right.

The car did, of course, have its failings. The engine noise beyond 5500 r.p.m. became quite intrusive, and there was a sharp fall-off of power at about the same point in the engine's speed range. The handling was also not quite flawless; provided that the road surface was smooth, there were no problems, but hitting a pothole in mid-bend would have the rear end of the car skittering and hopping quite badly — I can still remember one particular tussle with an RS 2000 when I clipped a pothole right on the apex of a bend. I was travelling at a quite illegal speed, and had a devil of a job to avoid piling the car into a ditch, such was the force with which the rear axle was thrown off line. The car could also feel decidedly slow if much use of the gearbox wasn't made; trying to pull away again after slowing with the tachometer showing much under 3000 r.p.m. or thereabouts, and it seemed to take an age before the car started to pull properly. The last criticism was that the brakes showed a distinct tendency to fading after a series of high-speed stops.

Altogether the car was in production for a little over a year in right-hand drive form, and in that time only about 1,500 examples were built — a total of about 3,500 (accurate figures have never been available from Ford) cars rolled off the production carousel at South Ockendon/Aveley, but the balance were left-hand drive models destined for Germany. In that time, short though it was, the RS 2000 managed to eclipse the Mexico and the RS 1600 — which must have upset certain members of Ford's marketing department. The ideal was to steal sales from other manufacturers, not from themselves! That this occurred is

hardly surprising, though, as all but customers who intended their cars to have a competition life would fall for the extra comfort and sophistication of the 2000 compared with the RS 1600, and potential Mexico buyers would find themselves seduced by the additional power of the RS 2000, for such a small premium in price.

When Ford introduced the re-bodied Escort in 1975, it was made obvious that the RS 2000 concept would be carried over into the new set of clothes. It was, however, some nine months before the car actually went on sale in Britain, and there was a fundamental difference between this and earlier RS cars in that it was not built up at F.A.V.O., but was in fact a mainstream production model being built alongside lesser Escorts at Saarlouis in Germany, as by this time South Ockendon/Aveley had been mothballed, a casualty of the oil crisis — the plant had never been able to come anywhere near the mainstream production facilities in Germany or at Halewood in terms of profitability. This is hardly surprising, as constructing a Mk I RS 2000 involved painted and part-trimmed, glazed and wired Escort bodyshells being shipped by road from Halewood, near Liverpool, down to the east side of Essex. Engines were built on a sub-contract basis for F.A.V.O. by a number of suppliers in the home counties, and the cars were completed on a labour-intensive carousel line.

The revised bodyshell of the Mk II Escort was intended only as a stopgap measure, with production planned only until 1990, when the new World Car (code-named Erika, but known to us as the Mk III Escort) would be ready to go into production. In an effort to make the car look as different as possible from its predecessor, Ford's stylists made use of sharp, angular lines which featured a slab nose that was about as aerodynamic as a housebrick. In fact, the Mk II Escort was appreciably worse, aerodynamically, than the Mk I version of the car had been. In an effort to overcome this for the prestige model in the line-up, a wedge-shaped nose section was designed and fitted to a prototype of the car, which was then wind-tunnel tested. The combination of this and the small bootlid spoiler was enough to clip 16% from the drag co-efficient — but that was only enough to restore the ability of the car to cut through the air as cleanly as a Mk I Escort had been able to. And they call it progress ...

But for all of its aerodynamic shortcomings, the second generation of RS 2000 was a striking and attractive car. The new nose cone was made up from a deformable plastic material, able to withstand many of the little knocks and scrapes that can occur whilst parking — it was the same material that bumpers on European cars destined for the American market were made

from. The rear spoiler on the RS 2000 was made from the same material. As was common with cars of the period, attempts had been made with the second generation of Escort to save weight, mostly by the use of thinner sheetmetal and reduced structural reinforcements, but on the RS 2000 the additional body fixtures and reinforced suspension pickup points were enough to ensure that the final car was, in fact, something like 70 lbs heavier than its predecessor.

To counter the additional weight, Ford's engineers redesigned the rather agricultural exhaust system that had been fitted to the Mk I RS 2000, and this gave a gross power increase of 12 b.h.p. The nett increase of the new generation car's power unit was brought back down to 10 horsepower, though, because the newer car used an engine-driven fan in place of the electric unit that space had dictated on the Mk I version of the RS 2000. The combination of aerodynamic aids and extra power were enough to ensure a slight improvement in performance — the Mk II could achieve 112 m.p.h., and could make the 0-60 run in about 8.7 seconds.

The tradition of a high trim specification was carried over, for a short time at least, onto the Mk II version of the car. However, in 1978 Ford's marketing people reappraised the car, and decided that henceforth there would be two levels of trim available; the

basic, which had the interior specification of the Mexico, and the Custom, which came with a centre console, a pair of Recaro front seats, and one or two other items such as tinted glass, a remote-control door mirror, and a glovebox. From this point the basic car came with steel wheels, with only the Custom pack-optional version having the familiar alloy rims.

By the time that the RS 2000 became available in Mk II form, Ford had got the suspension settings of the car just about right, and in the dry a specimen in the hands of a good driver will still prove a difficult car to beat. The response of the standard car's steering was precise, and if the particular example that you come up against has the RS option of the "fast rack", the driver is in control is a superb machine. Power output from the engine is more than adequate (and more than an XR3i), and the gearbox is sharper and more slick than any front-wheel-drive Escort production model. Ally these characteristics with the excellent brakes of the car, and you will see why the car is almost as desirable now as it was then.

As with the original model of RS 2000, there were plenty of options and extras to choose from when ordering a new RS 2000. ▷

RS 2000

◁ up to and including the Group One engine that resides under the bonnet of the yellow car that features on these pages. This example belongs to Peter Nixon, an official of the RS Owners Club, and is, as one might expect, in concours condition. Peter bought the car in early 1977 when it was less than a year old, and at present the car has covered less than 18,000 miles in total. The Group One engine was installed when the car had run up 16,000 miles, and features twin 44 IDF Weber carburettors under that

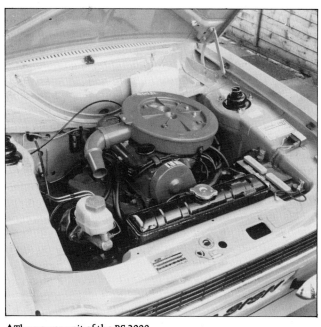

▲The power unit of the RS 2000 was the same in both cars — a tuned version of the Cortina 2.0 litre engine. In the Mk I it produced exactly 100 b.h.p.

massive air cleaner. A higher compression ratio, uprated camshaft, substantially re-worked oilways and careful building were adequate to ensure a power output at the rear wheels of 114 b.h.p. — which translates to something in excess of 140 b.h.p. at the flywheel. A Janspeed exhaust manifold with stainless steel system takes care of silencing. Other changes to the car include replacing the original equipment dampers with Ford-supplied Bilstein units, and the replacement of the original radio with a higher-grade stereo system.

Bodily, Peter's car is in totally original condition (aided by wax injection), and features a vinyl roof with Britax cloth sunroof. As might be expected, the performance is improved over that of the standard car, it being capable of 125 m.p.h., with a more brisk rate of acceleration.

The second generation RS 2000 is far less rare than the Mk I, as some 10,000 examples were produced before the final model

rolled off the line in 1980. Quite how many of these cars found their way onto the British market is unknown, but what is certain is that the prices being asked for the small number which seem to be offered for sale at any given time are creeping ever higher — we recently saw a late model example in very good condition, with a low mileage (about 35,000 from new) offered at £5,250. A tatty model in need of a complete re-spray and partial re-trim was commanding over £2,500 in the same issue of Exchange and Mart.

According to both of the owners whose cars are illustrated on these pages, the major difficulties encountered are firstly obtaining an authentic model, and then being able to get hold of trim items and chrome pieces. Paul Corkhill is himself able to supply authentic replicas of such pieces as the decal sets for not just the RS 2000 models, but also for other RS and Mexico items, and the RS Owners Club can assist with lots of small, difficult-to-obtain pieces, but it seems that such items as, say, a new fascia pocket or a rear quarter internal trim panel are increasingly difficult to obtain. One of our regular advertisers, Withers of Winsford, may be able to assist in this matter, with good-condition secondhand parts. It may also be worthwhile inserting a free small ad in the next available issue of **Performance Ford** stating the parts that you are looking for.

As regards the authenticity of the car itself, the key is to check the build number which is to be found on the metal plate attached to the front valance of the car, just to the side of the bonnet catch. In the case of a Mk I example, the first part of the number code should be the letters BAT (Britain, Escort Two door), with a fourth letter which denotes the year of original manufacture — 1973 is N, and so on through the alphabet. There will then be a space, followed by the designation G, which stands for RS 2000 or Mexico. Then comes another string of letters: B (Britain), F (South Ockendon — if the two letters are BB, then the car is not authentic, as that is the code for a Halewood-built car), A (Escort), T (Two-door), N (1973), and one other letter, which is a random-coding for the month of manufacture. Finally, there will be the five-digit chassis number of the car. The same system applies to the Mk II RS 2000 models, but certain letters would change — the B would become a G (Germany), and the seventh letter would become a C for Saarlouis. On the second line of the ID plate would be further details of the authenticity of the car; it should start off with 2 (for right-hand

This particular car is fitted with a Group One engine, which gave a substantially higher power output. ▼

drive), followed by NE for RS 2000. If it ain't got these references, it ain't a genuine car.

Because of the overall simplicity of the car, there is little different to check when looking at a used example of this car than there is on any model of '70s Escort. Some degree of noise from the rear axle and from the gearbox is far from unknown, but the clutch action should be reasonably sharp and precise, as should the steering gear. The major bugbear with the Pinto engine in its earlier forms was the poor lubrication to the camshaft, which led to rapid wear — any exaggerated ticking noise at idle speed which becomes proportionally quicker as engine speed increases is a sure sign of the first symptoms. Other than that, the engine should not be excessively worn, noisy or smokey.

The bodywork of the RS 2000 in its first incarnation is likely to hold up a little better than that of the later version, mile for mile on the clock, because of the greater strengthening and more substantial sheetmetal that went into the Type 49 shell. If at all possible, put the car that you would like to buy on a ramp, and closely inspect the underside of it, not just for rusting, but also for signs of damage — remember that many of the cars have, at some point in their lives, been used for some form of competition work, and not everybody carried out satisfactory repairs. If a ramp is unavailable, lift the carpets and inspect the floorpan closely. The same degree of attention should be given to the front outriggers at the base of the inner wings and to the front bulkhead, for similar reasons.

One or two people have baulked at the prospect of buying cars that weren't quite as the textbooks said that they ought to be, but it is worth remembering that small detail changes were often made, particularly at South Ockendon, to cars which would perhaps start their lives as press demonstrators, or as

CONTACTS

Paul Corkhill,
0253 697552.
(RS decal kits to OS specification. Also aluminium RS Mk I spoilers.)

Withers of Winsford,
Department P.F., Wharton House, Wharton Road, Winsford, Cheshire CW7 3BY.
(Specialist supply of genuine RS parts.)

Adrian S. Flux,
0553 765450.
(Specialist motor insurance schemes.)

models for photographic purposes. Then there were the many RS options that could be added to a car, either during production, or at a later date. These could be anything from a set of Cibie spotlights to a Salisbury limited-slip differential unit. The final piece of advice that we can offer to the person contemplating the purchase of an RS 2000 for the first time is to consult the RS Owners Club — they are often able to offer all manner of good advice, and may even be able to find a local member who would assist you in your search — see the separate section on the club for details of how to contact them, and the services that they can offer.

Having actually obtained a good example of the marque, the owner is left with just one more problem: hanging onto the car. Because the locks used on all but the latest Fords are about as secure as a papier maché padlock, Escorts in general and RS 2000s in particular have an awful tendency to disappear. Therefore, retention of your property should become a major priority. Start by adding a good alarm system — one with an ultrasonic system, backed up by microswitches to the bootlid and bonnet. Then add a set of Yale or Kaba additional doorlocks — the Mk II featured here has these fitted, and they are tidy enough not to upset the immaculate lines of Peter Nixon's car. Finally, invest another few pounds on a set of locking wheelnuts — those F.A.V.O. alloy wheels are becoming rare, and thus increasingly prone to disappear. Of course, a professional car thief will be able to get past any alarm system or set of additional locks, and so be certain that you are not only adequately insured, but also that your policy covers the actual (rather than book listing) value of the car. Adrian Flux are able to offer the appropriate advice on which type of policy is best suited to your needs.

THE RS OWNERS CLUB

Founded in 1980, the RSOC is the only club which caters purely for owners of Ford Rallye Sport cars, from the Escort Twin Cam through to the RS 500 Cosworth, plus feature RS models as they appear.

Membership stands in excess of 2,500 members, and in return for their annual subscriptions members receive a package of benefits which include discount schemes for parts, insurance and recovery schemes, and special offers on club clothing and insignia. Then there is an excellent bi-monthly club magazine "Rallye News", which is packed with useful features, a very active correspondence section, details of special offers, advertisements, and much more.

Then there are the many events which the club organises for its members. These vary from national racetrack days to national gatherings and concours events, through to appearances at classic car shows and local events. Each area throughout the country has local centres, and the various models covered by the membership are also given their individual membership registers.

Finally, the club is actively involved in the sourcing and supply of many of the hard-to-find parts that are no longer in production.

For full details of the many benefits that are available, to both RS owners and non-owning RS enthusiasts, contact the Membership Secretary at the RS Owners Club, Department P.F., 80 Reepham, Orton Brimbles, Peterborough PE2 0TT.

RS MEXICO II

A new bodyshell — but a poor reception

The Escort Mk II Mexico — the only car to be sold as an RS Mexico — is best described as Ford's Nearly Car. On paper, it combined the best of both worlds, sharing the RS 1800's bodyshell with a neat, reliable, and reasonably powerful 1600 overhead cam engine. It ought to have been a success — it had good handling, quite reasonable performance, and the coveted RS tag as an aid to credibility. It was only the timing which was wrong.

The original Mexico had been conceived as a cheaper alternative to the RS 1600 and RS 2000, and was by a long way the single most successful RS car in terms of sales. However, when the Escort range was re-shelled in 1975, there were four cars pencilled in to fill the rôles of three in the previous range. For out-and-out competition work, there was the BDA-engined RS 1800. For fast road and club level rallying there was the RS 2000, the most distinctive of all Mk II Escorts with its droop snout nose cone. Next down the line came the RS Mexico, and then at the bottom of the range was the Escort Sport, which made use of the Kent crossflow engine in a choice of 1300cc or 1600cc sizes.

The Mexico's problem was that it fell between two stools; it wasn't that much quicker than the 1600 Sport, and the RS 2000 was a substantially faster and more glamorous car. In terms of price, at the time of the launch in January 1986 the RS 2000 cost £2,400, the RS Mexico £2,090, and the 1600 Sport £1,650. And what happened was that customers either went for the 1600 Sport, which was a bargain by the standards of the day, or the RS 2000 which gave scintillating performance for a price which was still well within reach. The Mexico derivative of the Mk II Escort was left out in the cold, and ceased production just 34 months after the first example had rolled off the line at Saarlouis in West Germany. It wasn't just the buying public who ignored the Mexico either — even many of the magazines of the day failed to get hold of examples for test.

I was fortunate enough to have been able to sample a privately-owned example of the RS Mexico, and remember it being a surprisingly pleasant machine — and reasonably nippy to boot.

Mechanically, the RS Mexico was quite simple. The bodyshell was the standard two-door Escort II item, with a small amount ▷

RS MEXICO II

◁ of stiffening added to the front and rear damper mountings, and the same grille and bumper arrangement as that seen on the RS 1800. Under the bonnet was to be found a 1593cc version of the American-designed Pinto single overhead camshaft engine, with substantially oversquare dimensions of 88mm bore x 66mm stroke — neither dimensions were shared with the RS 2000's externally-similar engine which had a bore of 91mm and a stroke of 77mm. A specially-designed exhaust system was used on the Mexico, and this combined with the Weber DGAV twin-choke and a compression ratio of 9.2:1 to produce a mean power output of 95 b.h.p. @ 5750 r.p.m. Torque was rated at 92 lb/ft @ 4000 r.p.m.

Backing up the engine was the same four-speed transmission that was to be found in the RS 2000. The rear axle is another component shared with the RS 2000, complete with the 3.54:1 final drive ratio. A two-piece propshaft joined the two parts of the driveline.

The suspension system was fundamentally the same as that to be found beneath all Escort Mk II cars, with a MacPherson front end and leaf-sprung rear. Double-acting hydraulic telescopic dampers were utilised at each end of the car, with 10.5" (free length) 130 lb front coils, and triple-leaf semi-eliptical 115 lb rear springs. The rear axle had location aided by a pair of forward-facing radius arms, and at the front an anti-roll bar was used to give longitudinal location. A 3½ turn lock-to-lock steering rack completed the picture on the standard car — although a 2.5 turn

rack was an option on the car. Brakes were solid 9.7" discs on the front hubs, 9" x 1¾" drums on either end of the rear axle, and servo assistance was provided.

The interior of the RS Mexico was best described as functional. Much use was made of matt black paintwork, plastic, and carpeting throughout — all very sporting on paper, but rather claustrophobic in practice. A pair of fixed-back cloth-faced front seats, which hinged on their leading edges to allow access to the similarly-trimmed rear bench seat were to be found inside, as was an RS three-spoke steering wheel. Ahead of the steering wheel was a neat instrument binnacle which housed a 7000 r.p.m. tachometer and 140 m.p.h. speedometer, with three tiny gauges squeezed between them to monitor oil pressure, water temperature and fuel tank contents. The reason for the apparently optimistic maxima of the speedo and rev counter was that the same cluster was also used not only on the RS 2000, but also the competition-intended RS 1800. The instrument cluster, incidentally, was the recipient of a Design Award for its clarity — even though its single glass pane was an idea neatly poached from BMW. To the credit of the designers involved, the panel still looks reasonably contemporary — it is only the oil gauge, which for some reason is no longer considered a necessity on factory-produced Fords, which gives away the age of the design.

> "The Mexico's problem was that it wasn't that much quicker than the 1600 Sport, and the RS 2000 was substantially faster and more glamorous."

Performance of a standard RS Mexico was reasonably nippy, but far from earth-shattering; the benchmark 0-60 run could be managed in about eleven seconds, and the car could eventually achieve a maximum speed of just over 100 m.p.h. Even though the Pinto 1600 produced seven more horsepower than the Kent 1600 of the earlier Mexico, the car was appreciably slower in terms of acceleration than its predecessor — this was directly

attributable to two factors, the principal one of which was the gaining of about 150 lbs weight when the new bodyshell was introduced. The other cause was that for all of its contemporary styling, the Mk II car cut through the air about as effectively as a housebrick — the drag coefficient of the Escort Two was 0.45, whereas the original Escort Mexico achieved a far more aerodynamic 0.425.

The engine's power output, fortunately, could be easily increased; just adding a pair of sidedraught Dellorto or Weber carburettors and a less mild camshaft would be enough to show a nett power increase of twenty five or even thirty per cent. A Mexico with an engine thus-equipped would be able to turn in performance figures close to those of an RS 2000, which can make the 0-60 run in 8.7 seconds and manage a maximum 112 m.p.h. A major advantage of the RS Mexico was that the car was engineered to take up to 140 b.h.p. without any problems, and so a substantial amount of tuning could be carried out before any of the driveline would begin to show signs of strain.

That the Mexico is underpinned with a suspension system designed by Ford Rallye Sport becomes apparent the first time that a driver points the car towards a stretch of winding road. The RS philosophy has always been to endow their cars with sharp handling, excellent roadholding, and constant feedback to the driver, and they were as successful with the RS Mexico as they were with all of their other projects. With the suspension settings at their factory rates, the car remained surprisingly neutral in its road attitude; there was no tendency towards either oversteer or understeer providing the correct amount of power was being fed through to the tarmac. As with any rear-wheel drive hot Escort, lifting off the throttle in mid-bend would have the back end of the car snapping outwards, and it was also essential to keep cornering speeds down to a prudent level whenever the roads were wet.

Such was the feedback to the driver from the four corners of the car — through the seat of the pants as well as via the steering wheel — that it would take a particularly insensitive or ham-fisted driver to bring a Mexico to a sticky end. As with any RS car, it responded best to being driven lightly, and the weighting of the controls were encouraging in this respect; the steering wheel never became either over-heavy or feather-light, and the pedals were well-spaced, of equal height, and immediately responsive. Finally, this was one of the last generation of Escorts to be graced with the short-throw, knife-through-butter gearshift.

The car was not, of course, totally viceless in its handling. The cart-sprung rear axle could be skittish when driving along uneven roads, and a pothole encountered in mid-bend would be enough to re-direct the car from its chosen path. The brakes could tend to fade after repeated applications within a shortish distance, and the car was rather tyre-sensitive; different makes could totally transform the roadholding characteristics. Lastly, the lack of power could become frustrating on a fast run, as the driver became increasingly aware that the chassis could be pushed a lot harder than the engine would allow.

Getting hold of a genuine RS Mexico nowadays is not easy, primarily because so few were built — records indicate that only 2,200 were produced in the car's lifetime, which is put into sharp perspective by the ten thousand-odd RS 2000s which made their way onto the British market during the span of the Mk II Escort's life. Fortunately, because the Mexico was principally a road, rather than a competition, car, a better-than-expected percentage have survived, and they are now appreciated as having Collectors' Car status.

By far the best source for obtaining a good example of the car is the RS Owners Club — whilst cars do not come up for sale very often, those that are advertised in the R.S.O.C. magazine will

certainly be authentic, and the prices asked for them seem to be a darn sight more realistic than for certain RS Mexicos that have been advertised recently in one of the quality Sunday newspapers! Indicative of the scarcity of these cars is the fact that of more than 1,600 Mk II Escorts owned by R.S.O.C. members, only 224 were Mexicos, at the end of October last.

Checking the authenticity of a Mexico is not that easy, but the first check should be of the Vehicle Identity Number, the plate for which lives on the right hand side of the front valance panel ▷

RS MEXICO II

adjacent to the bonnet catch. This ought to start with the letters BFAT, and fifth letter either S, T, or U — although there may be one or two examples about with the letter R as the fifth part of the code. That is because the letter refers to the year of manufacture, R being 1975, S 1976, and so forth. Production actually started in the last couple of months of 1975, although no cars were offered for sale until January 1976. The last example rolled off the production line at Saarlouis in September 1978, and was registered before the end of the same year.

Because of its predominant use as a road, rather than competition, vehicle, it is likely that any examples being offered for sale will be substantially of original specification. It is quite possible that the engine could have been uprated, and also that the dampers have been replaced with more effective gas-controlled items; the original equipment oil-filled units are prone to aeration when used a lot (such as on a fast run), whereas gas-filled items retain their design efficiency for much longer.

The only other changes that a prospective purchaser is likely to come up against are likely to be on the inside of the car, where additional items of comfort could well have been added. Whilst they looked very good, those fixed-angle bucket seats would not suit everybody, and a favourite swap amongst owners of Mexicos was to replace the original pair with the reclining Recaro seats from an RS 2000.

Keeping a Mexico on the road is quite easy, as virtually all its components are still available from the factory. Notable exceptions are inner wings, and strut reinforcement plates, which owners now have to replace by using modified versions of standard Escort items. The one remaining difficult area of parts availability concerns that major bugbear of anybody driving a pre-'80s Ford; trim panels. Some pieces are still available, but the golden rule if you intend to ever show the car in a concours d'elegance is to guard the soft bits within your car's cabin from all possible sources of harm.

> "As with any other hot rear-wheel drive Escort, lifting off the throttle in mid-bend would have the rear end snapping outwards."

Finally, the Mk II Escort in general, and the RS derivatives of the range in particular, lie prone to that scourge of the '80s, the car thief. This is due in no small part to the ease with which the standard locks on the car can be broached. I would therefore suggest in the strongest possible terms that the car be treated to a high-quality alarm system, and a set of high-security deadlocks on the doors and bootlid. By taking such a measure, you at least stand a chance of hanging on to a car which is surely heading towards the status of collectible.

NTV 580 P

The subject of a recent total rebuild, Mark Slater's immaculate Mexico is a perfect example of Ford's policy of "continued development". The first thing that struck me on seeing the car was that the door handles and window trim inserts were in a chrome finish — whereas virtually every RS Mk II car had black pieces of trim. Yet those chrome items were totally original, and Mark was able to bear out their authenticity by showing me an original sales brochure from the beginning of 1976, which showed both a Mexico and an RS 2000 thus-equipped.

Mark bought the car a couple of years ago, from a person who had left the car garaged and undriven for some eight years. The car was in "a bit of a state" due to not being properly stored, but Mark set to on a restoration programme which has resulted in the car you now see in front of you. The mileage registered on the car is under 30,000, of which Mark has clocked up about 3,000 in his period of ownership. The car was built in mid-1976, and was delivered to its first owner in October of that year. Mark, from Timperley in Cheshire, is only the second owner of the car, and understandably has no intention of parting with his superb example of Mexico, which is totally standard save for the RS 2000-pattern reclining seats which were a factory-fitted option installed at the original owner's request.

RS 1800

A rally car in a quiet lounge suit

With one or two noticeable exceptions, the department responsible for turning out competition versions of Ford of Britain's cars always has to work within the confines of a very tight brief. The team at Boreham are expected to take a designated model of car and turn it into a rally and race-winning machine, but without expending vast amounts of time or money — and they also have to ensure that the finished product bears a close resemblance to the production model upon which it is based. After all, Ford's involvement in motorsport has no pretence towards philanthropy — their factory-backed teams compete solely to generate interest in the regular production models which are offered in their dealerships.

Given the constraints under which the Boreham engineers and designers work, it is little short of miraculous that they have managed to produce as many winning cars as they have over the years — yet they consistently succeed, against the odds.

In the middle of 1972 the Mk II Escort was "signed off" — Ford parlance for final approval prior to making the necessary production tooling — and shortly afterwards Boreham started to research the competition potential of the forthcoming car. To

succeed, it was decided, they would have to develop on the theme of the all-conquering RS 1600 Escort — a car which had already carved itself an enviable reputation amongst both motorsport competitors and road users. Fortunately for the team responsible, the new car would be based around the floorpan of the Mk I Escort which meant that many of the existing pieces already developed for the RS 1600 could be carried straight over to the Mk II car — saving precious resources.

The BDA Cosworth engine which was to be found beneath the RS 1600's bonnet was tried and tested, and so was a natural choice of powerplant for the new car. However, an impending change in the international competition class rules led Ford to change the dimensions of the engine, increasing both bore and stroke, and thus overall displacement. A crankshaft of 77.62mm throw was installed (this was the same as that found in the standard Escort engine, should you think that the dimension sounds familiar), and the all-aluminium alloy block was bored out to 88.75mm which resulted in a capacity of 1835cc. The head was, to all intents and purposes, the same as that which had seen such sterling service on the RS 1600 block, being a 16-valve item with its twin overhead camshafts driven by a belt from the crankshaft.

In competition form the engine could put out something like 275 brake horsepower, but such a musclebound unit would find few friends on the street, and so it was decided that Brian Hart would be handed the project of modifying the BDA for road use. Working in the opposite direction to his usual modus operandum, Hart replaced the camshafts with a pair of much milder dimensions, lowered the compression ratio of the unit to 9.0:1 by installing revised pistons, swapped the exhaust manifolding for a simple-but-effective cast affair, and in place of the usual twin Dellorto or Weber 48mm sidedraught carburettors used a single 32/36 Weber DGAV downdraught on a restrictor manifold. Valve sizes were set at the same as those of the RS 1600, with 31mm inlet pairs and 27.4mm exhaust, and ▶

RS 1800

with lift limited to 8.75mm. The result was a power output of 115 b.h.p. @ 6000 r.p.m., and a useable 126 lb/ft of torque at 3750 r.p.m. — although the latter figure was occasionally given by the factory as 120 lb/ft @ 4000 r.p.m.

If the engine was distinctly mild by competition standards, the rest of the car was set up ready to roll onto racetracks and rally stages with a minimum of alteration. The gearbox had the same basic casing as other RS inline Escorts, but came standard with a closer set of ratios which enabled the most to be made of the high power outputs which could be gained from the engine by reversing the work carried out by Brian Hart. Fortunately, the ratios chosen also worked extremely well with the torquey standard road engine, so non-competition-orientated RS 1800 owners did not suffer. A cable clutch with a driven plate of 8½" fed the power from the flywheel to the transmission. Whilst the close-ratio four-speed was fine for road use, incidentally, the factory rally team eschewed it in favour of a stronger and more useful ZF five-speed unit.

Under the rear of the car lived a front-loader Timken-type axle of the variety found under other RS Escorts, with the same 3.54:1 final drive as the Mexico. This was suspended from the body via a pair of three-leaf springs, working with Bilstein twin-tube dampers and a pair of forward-facing radius arms — although quite a proportion of the cars offered for general sale used Girling dampers, and some even had Armstrongs fitted from the factory. At the front of the car were a pair of MacPherson struts, with either Bilstein or Armstrong damper units, working with 10½" coil springs rated at 130 lbs. Rear spring rates were 115 lb units, in the interests of having the car handle basically neutrally, with eventual understeering characteristics.

The braking system was decidedly modest by modern standards, having solid discs of 9.7" at the front, 9" drums at the rear, and servo assistance — that part of the system living inside the car, just ahead of the front passenger as space beneath the bonnet was rather limited once the engine was fitted with its competition carburettors and exhaust system. For all of its conservative specification the braking arrangement proved itself to be quite satisfactory for normal road use. However, those choosing to use the car in competition immediately threw away the entire system, replacing the front discs with 9½" ventilated items effected by AP four-pot racing calipers and fitting solid discs to the rear axle instead of the drums. There was an adjustable front-rear bias built into the competition system, via a twin-cylinder pedal block with bridge bar, and no servo assistance. Apparently this system was pretty horrible when cold, but when the car was hot and running hard it was the only way of guaranteeing fade-free stopping power on a demanding rally course or racetrack.

The bodyshell of the standard road version of the RS 1800 was essentially the same as that of the lesser Escort RS Mexico — an unsurprising fact, given that the entire production run of

> "Contemporary road tests of the RS 1800 when it first appeared all had the same sentiments writ large — the car was overpriced and underpowered."

BDA-powered Mk II Escorts were built as Mexicos, prior to having their 1600cc Pinto engines and transmissions removed and replaced by the more businesslike set-up. The swapping was carried out by members of the Competitions Department first at the Pilot Plant at Aveley, and later at Halewood. Officially the

▲The Cosworth BDA was re-specified by Hart Racing for road use, and produced a modest 115 b.h.p. With revised cams, new pistons, and extra carburation (in this case a pair of 48 DCOE Webers), 220 b.h.p. is easily achieved.

RS 1800 was claimed to have been given an uprated rear damper mounting crossmember, but this has never been substantiated – of the RS 1800s which I have seen and tried, all have what look like stock Mexico damper mounts.

Externally, there was nothing more than a change of decals to identify that the car under scrutiny was an RS 1800, and not a Mexico; the front spoiler was the same as that of the lesser car, and the rear spoiler too was often found on production Mexicos. Round headlamps (additional lighting meant additional cost to the initial purchaser), quarter bumpers, and black bodywork trim were also shared with the Mexico, as were standard wide steel wheels.

Contemporary road tests of the RS 1800 when it first appeared all had the same sentiments writ large; the car was overpriced and underpowered. There was more than a grain of truth to both, but what seemed odd was that everybody responsible for testing the cars seemed to miss the point; it wasn't what the car was, but rather what it could be made to be that was its raison d'être. Costing something like half as much again as the Mexico upon which it was based, and with performance which was little better than the appreciably cheaper and less temperamental RS 2000, the £2,990 RS 1800 did, on paper, seem an extravagant way of buying a hot Escort.

However, the point of the car was that a clubman competitor could go out and buy an RS 1800, and without spending vast amounts of money turn it into a car which would neatly trounce the competition. For example, the standard version of the car would achieve the 0-60 sprint in about nine seconds, and would go on to exceed 110 miles per hour. A few hundred pounds' worth of engine bits later, the acceleration to sixty could be as little as six seconds, and the top speed may have risen to more than 120 miles per hour. Neither of the other two RS Mk II Escorts could have their performance transformed anything like as easily. In fact, it is unlikely that an RS 2000 could ever beat an 1800 in competition, such is the relative potential of each car.

As well as being able to easily extract substantial gains in power from the engine for relatively small amounts of cash, the buyer was also able to take full advantage of that great RS facility of a truly massive range of alternative and inexpensive chassis

option availability. The format of the car was simple, and a tremendous choice of springs, dampers, steering racks, wheels and tyres was on offer via the nearest RS dealership – as well as at dozens of performance parts retailers up and down the country. Roll cages, optional final drive ratio gear sets, safety equipment, you name it, it could be supplied for the RS 1800.

Being homologated for competition use normally involves a manufacturer in building a minimum number of cars which must be offered for sale to the general public – hence the availability in recent years of 5,000 RS Cosworths, a similar number of Mk I RS Turbo Escorts, 200 RS 200 models, and so forth. With the RS 1800, Ford neatly sidestepped that stipulation – with the consequence that there were apparently only 109 examples of the car built and sold, all in the U.K. market. How Ford did it was to ride on the back of existing approval for their earlier twin-cammed Escort, the RS 1600. Firstly the company used the Evolution rule to have the 1835cc version of the BDA approved for use in the RS 1600 – the engine was substantially the same, with officially only a differently-sized crankshaft used. They then managed to convince the relevant sanctioning bodies that the new Escort was, in fact, no more than a revision of the styling – the two cars were, Ford claimed successfully, substantially the same vehicle with no more than cosmetic changes.

Had Ford been unable to get away with that particular bit of rule-stretching and bending, then they would have been forced to make a thousand examples of the RS 1800 before it would have been accepted for competition in FISA Group 2. As it was, the car was added to the list of eligible cars as a variation on the Mk I Escort RS 1600, which was already on the list. Just to be on the safe side, the company built a few cars and offered them for sale through the RS dealership network. They even went as far as giving two options, the standard car, or the Custom version which had a more comprehensive level of trim pieces such as a centre console and a carpet in the boot. It is understood that the great majority of the production run which were sold had the Custom pack option fitted.

Quite how many of the cars which were sold for road use have survived is not known. The RS Owners' Club has an amazing thirty six examples within their membership – a far higher ▶

Sitting low, the RS 1800 was the definitive wolf cub in sheep's clothing. Boosting the power and varying the suspension would turn it into a grown up wolf!

RS 1800

◄ proportion than might have been expected to have survived, considering that quite a number of the original production run have seen some form of competition service in their lifetime.

Identifying a genuine car is a tricky business – the vehicle identification plate will tell an inquisitive owner that the car is a Mexico. Given that Holbay Engineering produced several hundred of the Hart-specification Cosworth BDA engines (this could become a Who's Who of the performance Ford scene ...), it is quite feasible that there could be the odd counterfeit car out there somewhere. I would like to be able to report of a secret code stamped into a hidden corner of the car somewhere which will tell that the car under scrutiny is a genuine RS 1800, but regret that no such detail exists. Authentication is going to be a matter of checking as much history as exists on a car – the R.S.O.C. can probably help here, having more information on the background to these cars than any other single organisation.

Interestingly, according to my colleague Jeremy Walton's excellent book **RS: The Faster Fords,** a small number of cars were built with engines prefixed HRE. Owners of such cars obviously lead a charmed life, because somebody up there has smiled on them, making available a car which has a steel racing-specification crankshaft with twelve-bolt flywheel, instead of the six-bolt, nodular cast iron assembly of the rest of the run. The steel crank will achieve and sustain far higher engine speeds, and so is obviously a desirable feature.

Being a competition machine which was offered for sale as lip service to the Federation Internationale de l'Automobile's rules on such matters, creature comfort wasn't terribly high on the list of priorities at Ford. The fact is that the car was equipped only with the most basic of trim items, just sufficient to stop salesmen in dealerships from sulking too much. You wanted power windows, a sunroof, a nice big stereo system? Make your own arrangements. All that Ford were offering was a wolf cub in sheep's clothing. With a few pounds well spent it would grow up into a real wolf.

The car was disappointing to drive – it seemed to lack some of the extra something that had set its predecessor, the RS 1600, aside from the rest of the Mk I Escort range. I remember being quite underwhelmed by the RS 1800 at the time of its launch, but harboured a hope to try one out with a decent (or better still, indecent) amount of power on tap. It took fourteen years to achieve that ambition. Whilst en route to take the photographs of the car which you see on these pages, owner John Wooler casually tossed me the keys to the ignition and invited me to try out the machine for myself.

John acquired the car a few months ago, thus fulfilling a long-time desire to own an example of this rare RS – as often happens, a friend had once owned one and the seeds to do likewise had been sown back then. It didn't take John Wooler long to decide that the chassis could handle a lot more power than it was being given, and so the engine was despatched to Burton Engineering in Ilford, Essex, with a request that they extract some more of the engine's potential. By the time that the

unit returned to the Woolers' home in Surrey it was producing a far more acceptable 220 brake horsepower – and the nett result is that the car now goes like it ought to have done in the first place.

I was warned about moving off from a standstill, being told that I'd need to load the throttle before letting the clutch back out. Dialling in about two thousand revs I eased out the heavy clutch pedal – and promptly stalled. From then on 3000 r.p.m. from standstill was the order of the day, and I didn't stall again.

Burton having managed to get power up without sacrificing too much torque – apart from leaving standstill, the engine will pull happily from just under two thousand revs. The steering is heavy but sensitive, the clutch pedal needs a left leg like that of Arnold Swarzenegger when driving in traffic, and the brakes are likewise in need of a solid shove, but the car is less of a brute than I had expected.

When the roads are clear and the opportunity exists the car will lunge forward like a racehorse responding to John Francombe. The aural sensations of that rasping exhaust note and the roar of four Weber 48 DCOE chokes all drawing air are wonderful to any driver with red blood in the veins, and the car tingles in the unique RS manner. Gearshifting is the familiar click-click-click RS process, and the clutch, which feels heavy around town, assumes the rôle of an on-off switch and becomes just right for the car, in total sympathy with its character. Power rolls on in a steady, surging wave and is adequate to propel the car to sixty in the low six-seconds timespan.

It was possible to order up the RS 1800 with different final drive gears, and also with a limited-slip differential. John Wooler's car has the latter option, and this is of considerable use when launching hard from a standstill, effectively reducing wheelspin. As so often happens, the standard spring rates have been changed, the standard ride height being maintained but much stronger resistance, particularly at the rear of the car has been built into the chassis. The result is a car which is a shade more nervous on the entrance to a curve, and one which rewards over-zealous use of the throttle pedal with a desire on the part of the back of the car to overtake the front. Fortunately the steering rack is fast enough in its action to counter the tendency – a facility aided by the proclivity of the limited-slip differential to keep the car heading forward. Braking action is good, surprisingly so considering the relative simplicity of the system, and the car is altogether a delight to drive.

John Wooler agrees totally. He took the car back up to his native Northern Scotland recently, and was amazed by the precision with which the car could be made to negotiate very demanding roads in the area of Loch Ness. The car commands total attention at all times – there is nothing in the chassis which allows the driver to cruise gently, pottering along. Either the driver concentrates on the job in hand, or the car displays a desire to remodel itself on the nearest tree.

I have a sneaky feeling that the interpretation of the RS 1800 as owned by John Wooler is closer to the car which Ford's engineers would like us to have had before the marketing people stepped in – my knowledge of the way that Competitions Department work is that they would like us to have cars closer in character to those built for motorsport use. Unfortunately, the marketing department concerned feel that such machines are too radical, too anti-social ... too unsaleable? As John Wooler has proved, Ford did themselves a disservice by putting the RS 1800 on sale in the form that they did. It will also make the owners of quite a few hot hatchbacks wonder what-the-hell-was-that? as it blasts by, BDA happily chattering away.

John Wooler is contemplating selling the RS 1800, due to other commitments. If you would like to talk to him about it, contact him on 01-878 8018 (day), 01-960 5528 (evenings), or 0860 549146 (mobile).

●

RS 1700T
The great white hope — until the axe fell

DENNIS FOY

A nearly new car? A white elephant? However you care to describe it, the Ford Escort RS 1700T was a radical machine, when compared with the XR3 with which it shared its basic bodyshell. But was the car as radical as it first appeared to be? Or did the sum of the parts amount to nothing more than a sleight of hand trick by Ford's Competitions Department, to conceal the fact that there were major problems with attempts to build a serious motorsport version of the '80s Escort?

The RS 1700T made use of the same basic bodyshell as the Escort XR3, but there all similarity ended. Under the lightweight, Kevlar-laminated bonnet of the RS lived not a transverse 1.6 litre CVH engine, but a sophisticated Ford Cosworth BD-T mounted fore-aft in the engine bay. This, the latest development of the venerable twin-cam Cosworth engine which had first appeared in an Escort back in the early '70s, was a 1778cc turbocharged and fuel injected power unit capable of producing anything up to 350 b.h.p.

Whereas the XR3 was a front wheel drive car, the newcomer made use of a Porsche 924-style transaxle which combined a Hewland five-speed gearbox into the final drive unit. Part of the original concept was the inclusion of a Ferguson Viscous Coupling limited-slip differential, but apparently none of the very small number of cars which were built actually featured this in their specification. A torque tube joined the engine to the transaxle.

Holding the two principal components into place was a network of steel tubes, sheetmetal fabrications, and what remained of the original bodyshell; much of the original Escort metalwork had been chopped away in order to accommodate the engine and transaxle, and the steel framework was essential to restore adequate strength to the bodyshell. An essential part of the car's development programme was the need to save weight, and for this reason wherever it was possible to replace a steel panel with a Kevlar-laminated item, it was done. The first example of the car to be unveiled to the press was a staggeringly handsome and businesslike machine which featured widened wheelarches, a completely redesigned nose section, abundant NASA ducts, and a sculpted rear end treatment. However, these items added weight — even though they were lightweight mouldings — and by the time that the car was undergoing serious testing on Welsh rally stages in the winter of 1981/2 many of the styling pieces had been removed from the car.

The suspension system of the car was designed expressly to cope with arduous rally stages, and consisted of a set of four coil-over-strut legs, located in turrets at the top, and by wishbone links at the bottom. These wishbones, incidentally, were nothing more than Sierra pieces, showing once again Ford Boreham's commitment to using as many parts-bin pieces as possible on any car which they are developing. Disc brakes on each corner are de rigeur on any competition vehicle, and sure enough those items are to be found inside each wheel rim of the RS 1700T.

The entire RS 1700T programme was beset by problems right from its inauguration in 1979, partly by a set of conflicting interests within Ford of Europe (Boreham maintained an interest in rallying, whilst Germany's principal cause was circuit racing), and partly by a total inability for the company to produce a small-run project.

The crux of the matter was that with the decade drawing to a rapid close, Boreham had no future car in their grasp with which they could continue to achieve rally successes; the Escort Mk II was about to cease production, in readiness for the forthcoming Erika project, the first front wheel drive car to bear the Escort ▶

RS 1700T

name. That therefore meant that they could not continue to pour resources into the RS 1800 project, successful though the car undoubtedly was; after all, no matter how many wins that particular car would go on to achieve, it would not help sell front wheel drive Escorts — and selling cars out of showrooms is an essential part of the reasoning behind Ford having a Competitions Department at Boreham. What Boreham therefore had to do was to produce a version of the Erika which would enhance the newcomer's image by being a success in competition — and would lead directly to showroom sales of "ordinary" versions of the Mk III Escort.

It didn't take a lot of deduction on the part of Ford's excellent tam at Boreham to decide that they would be flogging a dead horse, attempting to win rallies in a modified version of the forthcoming Escort — unless they shifted away from the production car's front wheel drive format and 1600cc CVH engine. There was neither the time nor the budget available to the department to enable them to make a really successful FWD rally car — but if they were to marry together their existing rear wheel drive technology, a few of the newer ideas which had been discussed such as a transaxle for improved weight distribution and turbocharging for more power, and then wrap them up in a car which at least looked like the new car which would be appearing in dealership windows at the beginning of the next decade ...

Group B was the class chosen as that in which the RS 1700T was to compete, and under the existing rules the company had to build a minimum run of 200 cars. Once that number had been reached, Ford could build another 20 as Evolution models, which could be far more radical versions of the original model. And that production run proved to be the stumbling block for the entire project — whilst Boreham could, given enough time, make the machine into a potential winner, the tremendous costs involved in trying to fit out a section of the production line at Saarlouis tp produce complete cars which could be sold to the public proved an unassailable hurdle. Thre was more than one person at Boreham who was wishing that they still had the South Ockendon facility for the production of limited edition cars ...

In essence, the RS 1700T was nothing more than a further development of the RS 1800 Mk II in a bright new set of clothes, and had Boreham's team been able to concentrate their energies on making the competition car as successful as its components suggested it could be, then the car would have become a classic of its time. Unfortunately, such was the arrangement at Boreham that in addition to sorting out the competition version of the car, the same small team was also landed with the many problems of turning the programme into a successful road car as well!

The entire budget for the programme came from that allocated to Boreham, and had the team been able to concentrate on the mechanical aspects of the car — rally teams would be less than concerned with the overall appearance of the car if they knew that it would go as well as its specification suggested — then the RS 1700T programme may have succeeded. However, because the majority of the 200 cars built would be expected to go on sale through RS dealers in Britain and West Germany, the quality of external finish, trim and comfort equipment would have to be at least on a par with those of the ordinary Escort 1.3L or whatever it was that was parked next to the RS in the showrooms. Massive amounts of money can disappear as if by

magic when it comes to tooling up for production runs, and the RS 1700T took its slice; apparently some £100,000 alone went into the production of moulds for the various Kevlar panels of the car, to ensure that all 180 or so examples of the car which would be offered for general sale would be identical, and of a sufficiently high standard for general consumption.

As might be expected, the interior of the early prototypes were somewhat basic; they were, after all, pure rally machines, and so needed nothing more than a pair of Recaro glassfibre bucket seats, and a fascia with only the most essential instrumentation – the other bits would be custom-added by the rally team who would be running the car. However, for road use a level of trim similar to the old RS 2000 Custom would be the minimum that the public could reasonably expect. As the car was to be productionised, an unnatural amount of money and time went into trying to get the car up to the required standard. Another problem area was the glazing of the car; due to the thin shell doors, the driver or passenger would make contact with the outside world via a hinged porthole in the Lexan door lights – but a potential road customer could no more be expected to tolerate that than he or she could be expected to put up with the rest of the car's glasswork being replaced by Lexan held in place by blind rivets. Then there were things like the wired-on single-nut wheelhubs, the absence of "luxury" items like a heating system, and so forth. Eventually, the odds of ever getting all of these problems sorted out simply overwhelmed the chances of an RS 1700T ever going on sale in RS dealerships. At a product planning meeting in March 1983, the entire project was axed.

By the point of the towel being thrown in, something like a dozen examples of the machine had been built, and several of them had undergone arduous testing at the hands of such drivers as Vatanen and Blomqvist. At least one car was totally destroyed during testing, and another two of the few were apparently mothballed; one is somewhere at Saarlouis, and another is under a dustsheet in a corner of a Boreham workshop.

The remainder went out to South Africa, along with a collection of spares such as body mouldings, transaxles and engines. Mick Jones, one of Boreham's most talented mechanics, followed the project out to Port Elizabeth shortly afterwards, and under his expert guidance the car achieved a variety of successes in the thriving local motorsport scene.

It is an ex-Mick Jones car which is featured on these pages. Now in the hands of an enthusiastic and talented Clubman rally driver, Simon Nutter of Kendal, the white machine is substantially standard; 1778cc engine with Garrett T.03 turbocharger, Hewland Transaxle, and so forth. Simon bought the car in the later part of 1987, and has campaigned it in all manner of events since. He describes it as rewarding to drive, and surprisingly reliable in competition, despite the shortage of research and development which went into the original project; his first transmission ate itself on an early event, but fortunately the car came complete with a spare and it was possible to build up one complete, good transaxle from the two sets of components – a cautionary stripping down of the spare before installing it into the car showed evidence of metal fragments within its fluid.

Whilst the original concept called for the wheel nuts to be locked into place with tie-wire, the four on Simon's car had no such safeguard, and in consequence he and his team find it necessary to torque up each hub between rally stages. Forgetting to do this when a stage was brought to a temporary halt recently almost brought him and his co-driver to grief – within moments of being flagged clear to continue, they were aware of a complete wheel and tyre passing them on the nearside. It was theirs. That in its own right was not a major problem – the difficult bit was trying to find the missing nut and its locating collar. After a few minutes of retracing their track and feeling about in the total darkness they located the nut, but the collar was proving elusive. Simon thought that he had found it at one point – only to discover that what he was feeling for in the grass ▶

RS 1700T

to the side of the track was, in fact, an unexploded small-arms shell. Given that they were on a stage through a military firing range area in the North East of England, they decided to abandon the search before they blew themselves up, and limped to the end of the stage with the nut held into place with a pair of Molegrips. What's that old adage about it being better to live and fight another day?

One area of the car which Simon has been forced to modify is the suspension. Nothing major, mind you, merely experimenting with various spring and damper rates. At the moment the car is running on what at first sight appear to be very strong (400+lb) front coils, but even these are proving a little soft, and the chances are that something closer to 500 lb pressure will prove about right.

As a club-level competitor, Simon has been able to run the car in a wide number and variety of events, but those days are rapidly drawing to a close — as the car was never homologated, it is increasingly barred from rallies. Because of this, Simon is offering the car for sale — its competition days are very definitely numbered, and Simon wishes to continue rallying, probably in a Group N machine. This is sad, because the chances are that A 170 RST (a totally authentic registration plate which will be sold with the car) will end its days as a road car, or as a museum piece; this is one of only three examples of the surviving few which is believed to reside in Britain, the other two being a black

one which is understood to be in nothing like the condition of this one, and the one that is under wraps at Boreham.

Wherever Simon has appeared with his car, it has been enthusiastically received, whether it was at an event, or at a place of special significance to the RS 1700T. For instance, he took the car down to Boreham during last summer, and was soon surrounded by members of the team who remembered the project fondly — although one wag was heard to mutter: "What's that doin' back 'ere? I thought we'd got shut of all them ..." Simon was also very impressed by the assistance he got from Hewland Engineering, when he was having his initial transmission problems; in addition to chatting on for some time about the car and the Hewland involvement in the project, the man from Hewland also sent Simon a full set of blueprints for the transaxle, thus enabling the rebuild to be carried out properly.

The only other modification which has been carried out on the RS was to the steering rack. For some reason best known to Ford, the chores of co-ordinating the action of the driver to the front road wheels are handled by a Saab 99 rack. This proved to have a standard, rather slow, action, and so another rack was obtained and modified to give a more immediate response. At present, it takes but two and a half turns of the steering wheel to take the road wheels from one lock to the other. When combined with the immediate engine response and the car's essentially neutral handling characteristics, it has made for a very positive, immediate, competition car. It is only a pity that the rules are changing to the point where it won't be able to realise its potential ... If you would like to give the car a good home, contact Simon care of **Performance Ford** at P.O. Box 14, Hazel Grove, Stockport, Cheshire SK7 6HL.

So is there really an answer to the rhetorical questions which start this feature? Was the RS 1700T old parts in a new set of clothes? Or was it good enough to have made the grade in its own right, as a member of the 1980s Escort line-up? Simon Nutter, along with Mick Jones and quite a few others, feel that had the Competitions Department at Boreham been able to get on and concentrate on developing the car for a purely competition future rather than as a semi-production car, then the car could have been a world-class competitor. Certainly it was the best of '70s format and '80s technology teamed together in one car. Where they probably went wrong was to try and pass off the concept as a version of the Mk III Escort, rather than as a damned good car in its own right. ●

RS 2800T

Zakspeed joins forces with Ford for the road

DENNIS FOY

During the later part of the '70s and into the '80s, the Capris of Zakspeed were virtually unassailable in the German **Gruppe 5** production modified Championship series. True, the cars conceived and prepared by Erich Zakowski bore little resemblance to the showroom cars with which they shared their name — they were built around a light-but-substantial spaceframe, clothed in a radically-altered set of clothes, and power came from a KKK-turbocharged Cosworth BDA of only 1427cc — but their success clearly encouraged a new wave of buyers to look at the Capri range in Ford dealers throughout Western Europe.

It is uncertain quite whose idea it was (presumably somebody in the marketing department of Ford of Germany), but Zakspeed is the name attached to the car which has become one of the rarest sights on British roads ever to wear the coveted RS tag — the Capri RS 2800 T.

Despite claims to the contrary, the car was conceived purely as a marketing exercise, in strictly limited numbers; the proposed 200 production run meant nothing in competition terms. All that it guaranteed was a scarcity value. Principally because of this, the car was overlooked by so many of Europe's motoring magazines — which was more than a little unfair, because the RS 2800 T offered a lot more than met the eye.

The basis of the car was the Capri 2.8 injection, which at the point of the appearance of the RS 2800 T had been on sale for just a year. However, instead of the 160 brake horsepower fuel injected engine, the RS used the basic 2.8 litre carburated engine of the then-current Granada range. The engine's basic power output was 135 b.h.p., but this was increased to a little over 188 brake horsepower by the addition of a turbocharger — initial studies were done using a KKK item, but this was later changed for a more reliable Garrett AiResearch turbo.

The system blew through a slightly-modified Granada 2.8 twin-choke Solex carburettor, which was set into a specially- ▷

RS 2800T

◁ developed airbox. Fuel was fed in by an electric petrol pump —
and the development team were most particular in pointing out
that there must be no filter between pump and carburettor! The
basis of the carburation system drew on the technology already
made available by the venerated Swiss engineer Michael May,
who has since gained greater fame for the work he has done
with Jaguar on their V12 HE engine. To cope with the additional
loads brought about by the turbocharger installation, it was
necessary to modify various engine components. Amongst the
list of changes were the installation of a Nitrided crankshaft, a
vibration damper for that component, an uprated lubrication
system, and more substantial head gaskets. The result of this
work was a smooth, free-revving engine developing
substantially more power than that of the 2.8 injection Capri.

It was a similar tale on the rest of the driveline, many parts being
similar to those found under the 2.8i Capri, but with subtle
changes here and there. For instance, although the braking
system was externally identical, that of the RS 2800 T had a
greater diameter bore on the master cylinder, and different brake
lines. The steering was also slightly different, mainly because
the engine mounts were different; to allow for this the steering
column of the RS was slightly longer, which called for a special
geometry setting.

Under the rear of the car was a limited slip differential, officially
an optional piece but which tended to appear on most of the
200 examples of the car ever built in Ford's Cologne factory. This
was set to a surprisingly high 75% loading — fifty per cent is a far
more normal rating to choose.

The front suspension system was much as that of the 2.8i Capri,
save for a marginally bigger front anti-roll bar and a set of
adjustable gas-filled dampers. At the rear, the system was
identical in all respects to that of the less-powerful production
line car. Wide steel wheels were the standard fitment for the car,
but an option was to have the car delivered on a set of 13" x 7.5"
RS alloy four-spoke wheels, just like those shown on the car in
our photographs. These were shod with 235/60 VR tyres. As a
space-saving move within the luggage area, the spare wheel was
a relatively skinny 5½" wide item, intended as a get-you-home
move until such time as the proper wheel and tyre could be
re-fitted.

To accommodate the wider rubber, Ford shipped the virgin
bodyshells out of their factory and across to Zakspeed's
premises, where the wheel arches and wings were treated to
some subtle flaring before the shells were returned to the
production line at Ford for the build-up process to continue.
Other vital differences in the visual appearance of the RS 2800 T
were a neatly-sculpted front spoiler, and a Ford Motorsport rear

▲ Power comes from a
turbocharged version of the
Granada carburated engine.

"A maximum speed of close
to 140 m.p.h. and a 0-60 time
of about 7.5 seconds seem to
be generally agreed."

The interior of the car used
Motorsport seats trimmed in a soft
grey velour. ▼

External differences from a Capri 2.8i were obvious; flared wings and special front and rear spoilers combined to give a very businesslike profile. ▶

aerofoil. Finally, there were "Turbo" badges on the bonnet, tailgate, and front quarters.

The interior of the car was similarly distinctive. In place of the usual Recaro seats normally found in top-line Capris, the RS 2800 T was fitted out with a set of superb Motorsport seats trimmed in the same soft grey velour as those inside the RS 1600i Escort of the same period. A leather-rimmed four-spoke steering wheel, co-ordinated deep-pile carpeting, door trims and fascia softwear completed the opulent look within the RS. Interestingly, there was no boost level gauge, as Ford felt that this would create unnecessary confusion for the driver.

From the moment that the car was fired up, its Rallye Sport heritage showed through – the car "tingled" just like all other RS cars. As with any turbocharged car it paid to let the car come up to its normal operating temperature before putting any weight on the throttle pedal, to ensure that lubrication was adequate to all moving parts. Once properly heated through the car could be opened up – and responded extremely well to a prod of the throttle!

So few of the cars were ever road tested by the press of the day that performance figures are not easy to come by; however, a maximum speed of close to 140 miles per hour, and a 0-60 time of about 7.5 seconds seems to be generally agreed, both of which show a reasonable gain over the Capri 2.8i. But more important than bald figures was the rate at which winding roads could be negotiated; keeping the power in and snicking up and down the gearbox would see the car devouring the bends and the miles in an effortless manner. The transmission itself was a standard 2.8i four-speeder, fitted with a shortened shift linkage to enhance the speed of changes, and this combined with an engine which suffered very little from "lag" (thanks to a high basic compression ratio of 9.2:1) enabled the car to make smooth, fast runs whenever bidden to do so.

Derek Speirs concurs with those sentiments. Derek, from Mansfield, is the owner of one of the three examples of the car which are believed to live here in Britain, having acquired the RS 2800 T from its original owner only three months ago after a lengthy period of persuasion. Finished in silver, and original in every respect but the red keyline stripes, Derek's car is fitted with the optional limited slip differential, which enables all of the power developed by the turbo-six to be put down to the ground very easily and tidily.

According to Derek, what sets the car apart is not so much its excellent straight-line acceleration – impressive though that undoubtedly is – as its phenomenal mid-range power; a squeeze of the throttle at virtually any speed is enough to have the car surging forward, lunging past whatever obstacle was in its way. The car feels extremely stable at all speeds, those big tyres grip superbly well in virtually all conditions, and the result is a surprisingly "user-friendly" car which constantly tells the driver what it is up to. The brakes work well, even if they lack "feel", but every Capri 2.8i owner will be familiar with that syndrome ... As with any other Capri, wet-weather driving is a cautious affair, with a marked tendency for the rear of the car to snap out of line all too readily, and so a gentle use of the controls is called for. However, in the dry the car can be pushed surprisingly hard.

Derek Speirs' car is in excellent condition throughout, and he intends to keep it that way. This ought not be too difficult to achieve, thanks to the number of shared components with the 2.8i Capri which are still readily available; it is only the special bodywork and trim items which could be problematic, and for that reason Derek is treating the car with the care and consideration that it deserves. Having said that, he doesn't "mollycoddle" the car, but takes it out and uses it hard whenever he feels like doing so. The Capri will also be putting in appearances at shows throughout the future.

Of the other two examples known to live within our Islands, not a lot is known. Derek Speirs went after one of them some time ago, but the car had been severely damaged and then badly rebuilt using a combination of Capri Ghia and 2.8i Special parts. The third car, a white one, was seen briefly in Brighton in 1985 by our own Ian Kuah, but has since disappeared from view. That third car, incidentally, was rumoured to have been brought over here for the use of one of the Directors of Ford of Britain, but we have been unable to substantiate the whispers. Which leaves Derek Speirs' car as the only example currently in use here in Britain with a full history. And he doubts that he will ever part with it ...

●

▲ The Zakspeed racing Capris which spawned the RS 2800 T.

RS 1600i

The first serious front wheel drive Escort

DENNIS FOY

When the Escort Mk III was introduced to Europe's motoring press at a lavish launch in 1980 (music by Vangelis, lighting by Genesis, and so forth), there was a conspicuous absence from the line-up of cars on display — there was no RS derivative. The word that filtered down from Ford's Public Relations Department was that the totally new concept of the Mk III Escort, with its front-wheel drive and previously unknown levels of passenger comfort, no longer aligned to the RS brand, and instead we were being offered the XR3.

As we were all aware, the RS tag had always been applied to cars which were destined for a career in competition, and at that point the feelings were that the future in racing and rallying lay with four-wheel drive or rear-wheel drive — certainly not cars which put the power to the ground via their front wheels. A number of us who were present at that event mourned the passing of the RS Escorts, but understood Ford's logic. We didn't realise at that point that Ford were, to paraphrase Sir Robert

Armstrong during the Spycatcher case in Australia, being "economical with the truth".

What was kept from us was that from a point a year or so earlier, Ford of Germany's Motorsport Division had already started developing a number of rather special versions of the front-wheel drive Escorts — cars which would eventually appear in the showrooms as the RS 1600i.

What prompted the move was the success of the Volkswagen Golf GTi — a car which Ford knew would outclass the XR3, even when the injected, five speed version of that car was ready in 1982. If Ford were to be able to continue to achieve success on the racetracks and rally courses of Europe with the Escort, they had to come with something substantially better than the XR3.

Using the three-door Escort with a 1600cc version of the CVH engine as a base model, their first move was to extract more ▷

RS 1600i

power. The standard CVH engine used hydraulic cam followers in the interests of quiet running and ease of maintenance. However, these act as a very effective rev-limiter, and preclude the engine from spinning at much more than 6200 r.p.m. — which is not a lot of use when a typical race car needs perhaps 8000 or more revolutions every minute. The car also needed a more radical camshaft than the standard 1600 and so a new set of profiles on the cam were chosen, and the shaft installed with a set of adjustable followers. To compensate for the greater valvetrain noise that the new lifters brought along with themselves, a cast-alloy finned valve cover was produced for the engine.

side, however, with the adoption of Bosch constant-feed electronic fuel injection, the same as that already to be found on the Golf GTi. This was the first factory installation of an injection system on the Escort, and proved so successful that it was adopted for the XR3 in 1983. The combination of these various engine modifications was enough to provide a mean power output at the flywheel of 115 b.h.p. @ 6000 r.p.m., with torque of 109 lb/ft at 5250 r.p.m. — a gain of something like 20% over the carburated XR3's engine. However, what the buyer got, as with all RS products, was a good starting point with masses of potential and it was possible to get as much as 160 or even 170 b.h.p. from the engine — a day spent port-machining the cylinder head, and tidying up the shapes within the ports, would yield perhaps ten or even fifteen brake horsepower.

A five speed transmission was considered essential on the car, and so it got one. This is virtually the same as that found in most current Escorts, with ratios similar to those of the XR3i. However, top gear was set at 0.76:1 on the XR3i, a figure which the Motorsport engineers decreed was "too tall". For the RS model fifth gear was set at 0.83:1. The final drive ratio of the car was also changed for the RS 1600i, to 3.84:1 — that of the XR3i was 4.27:1. The combination found on the RS 1600i meant that the car's theoretical maximum speed at its 6500 r.p.m. redline was 134 m.p.h. — although in practice, a standard car would not achieve any more than 120 m.p.h.

The next part of the engine to receive attention was the set of pistons; the standard 9.5:1 compression items were replaced with a new set which raised the ratio to 9.9:1. The bottom end of the engine is quite tough even in its standard form, and so that was left untouched. However, the standard exhaust manifold was less-than-successful in its ability to extract spent gases, and so a new casting was developed which was better able to get rid of the fumes from the head. The standard ignition system, too, was ditched in favour of a complex (some feel overly-so ...) flywheel-triggered, twin-coil distributorless system which had a rev-limiter in-built, which cut the sparks at 6500 r.p.m. Some owners of competition machinery have been known to dump this in favour of the original CVH distributor, suitably recalibrated to offer the desired advance curve.

The single biggest change to the engine was on the induction

Much of the development time of the RS 1600i — from starting the programme in early 1979, it took three years for examples to reach the showrooms — went into the suspension system. The standard Escort layout of MacPherson struts at the front end of the car was retained for the RS 1600i, but with a vital difference:

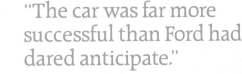

> "The car was far more successful than Ford had dared anticipate."

whereas the standard Escort utilises the anti-roll bar as a means of locating the fore/aft movement of the struts, that found on the RS does not. Instead, location was handled by a pair of links running between the track control arms and the car's bodywork. This freed the anti-roll bar, which was mounted via a specially cast alloy crossmember, to assume the sole rôle of additional springing.

At the rear of the car, the arrangement of struts, springs and swinging arms were supposed to be augmented by an anti-roll bar, if the literature of the day was to be believed. However, I have yet to see an example of the car which rolled off the production line with one fitted; it was offered as an optional extra on early specimens of the car, under part number 909-4599. It certainly improved those early examples — but more about that later.

The final parts of the car's mechanical specification were the same as the XR3; braking was taken care of by discs at the front and drums at the rear, with servo assistance achieved via a tortuous route across the bulkhead of the car. Steering was rack and pinion, unassisted. The only remaining difference found on the driveline of this car was in the area of the wheels and tyres. Those of the RS were substantially hunkier than anything hitherto seen on an Escort, being Ronal seven-spoke alloys (exclusive to Ford) in a size of 15″ x 6″, shod with 195/50 Dunlop D4 tyres.

Externally, the car was immediately identifiable. In addition to those big wheels and tyres, which filled the arches to perfection, the car also sat an inch or so closer to the ground than the XR3. Then there were specially-designed front and rear spoilers. Interestingly, it was the design of the rear spoiler which was a major contributory factor to the protracted birth of the car: to ensure that the car's entity was distinct, Ford decreed that the spoilers had to be very distinctive. However, that already found on the back of the XR3 was so effective at its job that most

> "It was the design of the rear spoiler which was a major contributory factor to the protracted birth of the car."

attempts at a replacement were less than successful. Eventually, however, the finished design was able to beat the XR3 item in terms of both drag and downforce. To complete the external appearance, a special decal set for both sides of the car, the bonnet and the tailgate were developed and applied.

The inside of the car was substantially better than the interiors of other, lesser, Escorts, primarily thanks to the grey cloth bucket seats and improved carpeting. Standard equipment was like so many other Escorts; pretty basic, until the options list was raided for such items as the sunroof and electric windows. A substantial four-spoke leather-rimmed steering wheel was, fortunately, a standard fitment — and very comfortable it was, too.

The car was, in its original form, something of a handful at speed through bends; few people would argue with the claim that the original rear suspension system in its basic format (that it, without the optional anti-roll bar) was a design disaster. What would happen would be that as soon as the power was applied, the rear wheels would start to steer the car. However, as soon as there was any change from a feed-through of power, they would start to "un-steer" and completely throw the balance of the car. The anti-roll bar tightened everything up rather nicely, and ensured that the wheels remained far more stable at speed. There was also a tendency for those big Dunlops to follow any available ruts in the road. This is not the fault of the tyre, but rather of the chosen size; even owners of current Escort RS Turbos, which have the same size rubber as standard, complain of the phenomenon.

What saved more than the occasional example of the early car

from being totalled in an accident was the directness of the steering; this was sharp and precise, and the driver was usually able to retrieve the car before matters got out of hand. The car's performance was more sparkling than its on-paper figures suggested, thanks to the free-revving nature of the injected engine; it was very easy indeed for a driver to run the car up to its electronic redline cutout, especially if it was a shade premature, and cut the power at, say, 6300 instead of the intended 6500 r.p.m.

To overcome these deficiencies, Ford's chassis engineers revised the suspension system of the car in the middle of 1983. The front struts, although still of Koni manufacture just like those of the earlier cars, were re-rated. To spot the difference between an early and a late example, the original cars had a strut top mount with twin bolts holding a plate to the turret, whilst later cars had a "sandwich" arrangement retained by a single locknut in the centre of the uppermost metal cup. At the rear of the car, the changes were more fundamental; the mainstream Escorts had all been redesigned in the areas of the swinging arm and tie-bar pivot points, the effect being to reduce dramatically the amount of positive camber shown by the rear wheels. The RS 1600i

shared this change, and the upshot was a car which no longer steered from the rear. At the same time there were other changes made to the car. A new, and bigger by seven litres, fuel tank was installed, along with a higher-capacity fuel pump — and for that reason the anti-roll bar offered for original specimens of the car would no longer fit the RS 1600i. Other changes included the substitution of a smooth velour for the crushed fabric on the seat and door trims, a slight alteration to the design of the mirror adjustment knobs, the deletion of the fascia lighting rheostat, and a new gearknob.

Those detail changes to the trim made little difference to the driveability of the car, but the suspension alterations transformed the behaviour of the RS 1600i. Running a late-model example hard through the bends became the pleasurable experience that it ought to have been in the first place, and there was a simultaneous whooshing sound to be heard throughout the City of London as a thousand insurance underwriters breathed sighs of relief.

The car was conceived as an homologation special, and Ford had ▷

RS 1600i

◁ intended to build no more than 5,000 of the machines, in order to qualify it for the international Group N classification of competition machinery. However, the car was far more successful than Ford had dared anticipate, and by the time that production stopped in 1983 more than 8,600 had been built, with demand still running as high as ever – it was only the imminent arrival of the first RS Turbo Escort which killed off the 1600i.

Despite quite a few reservations from both within and outside of Ford, the car became successful in competition. It placed quite well in a variety of rallies, particularly on tarmac, but it was on the racetracks that the car really shone. Running in Group A, with an engine pumping out in excess of 160 b.h.p., Richard Longman from Dorset came within a whisker of championship class wins in 1983 and 1984, the only full seasons in which the RS 1600i competed. Chris Hodgetts also raced an example with astounding success in 1985.

Of that production run of more than eight thousand, some 2,600 or so were built in right hand drive for the British market, the vast majority of which were registered in 1983. As you will gather from the earlier text, the best example to go for is a later example, which incorporates the revisions to the rear suspension system. However, having said that, an early model with the anti-roll bar added to the rear suspension (the part number is still listed on the RS parts computer, which means

A 448 MPU

Built in Saarlouis, West Germany during June 1983 and supplied new by Trimoco Chelmsford on August 1st of that year, the car spent the first two years and ten months of its life with its first private owner in Wickford, Essex.

The car was bought by its present owner, Jeff Mann, on 1st June 1986 with 34,040 miles registered. It has now covered a total of 38,901 miles. When purchased by Jeff it came complete with all documentation including the original sales invoice, and had been treated when new to the "total protection" wax injection programme.

The car is completely standard, except for a pair of Lucas "Bright Eyes" spotlamps, and higher-powered kick-panel speakers. It is fitted with seven of the nine available factory options, including the **very** rare Ford ESRT/32/PS digital stereo radio/cassette unit.

The main reasons that Jeff Mann gives for having purchased the car were that it was in an original and untouched condition of bodyshell and paintwork, it was totally rust-free in the area of the battery tray, it was a one-owner car, and the asking price was very reasonable indeed. Most of all, the fact was that when road-tested prior to purchasing, the car ran "as sweetly as syrup", a particularly noticeable characteristic of this post-May "facelift" model of RS 1600i.

that it is still available) is still a very desirable car.

As with so many RS cars, there are one or two imitators about; to establish if yours is the real thing, look at the trim details first – they should correspond to the seats shown in Jeff Mann's excellent example to be seen on these pages. Then look at the identification plate under the bonnet. If the code in the box for the engine says anything other than LZ it isn't the real thing – LR is an XR3i engine, and LU is a standard 1600 CVH. Remember, anybody can go out and buy a set of RS wheels and 1600i decals to convert their XR3i to at least look like the real thing.

Prices vary tremendously from one part of the country to another, and depend not so much on the age of the car, but more on whether the dealer is sufficiently clued up as to what the car actually is; those who know the scarcity of clean RS 1600i Escorts tend to ask the highest prices, whilst those who consider that they are selling a "tarted up XR3i" will be offering the car at a lower price. And that description is not my own – I actually heard a car dealer refer to an RS 1600i as just that, not too long ago. As a yardstick, I have seen one high mileage, slightly tatty specimen offered for just under £4,000, whilst a pristine example in a local main (but not RS) dealership was offered for a shade under seven thousand.

Insurance on these cars is on the steep side, as they are considered to be a Group 7 car – which is presumably why an increasing number of owners now garage their cars throughout the winter, and run them on a Classic Car-type policy for a restricted number of miles during the summer months. Whilst I can understand the financial logic of such an approach, I am afraid that I would find the temptation to go out and have fun in an RS 1600i too much to resist.

I was fortunate enough to be offered an extended run in a well-sorted example of one of these cars in 1983. An early model with the optional anti-roll bar on its rear suspension, the car had been treated to some strategic port re-working, and also had a Janspeed exhaust manifold. Power output was estimated at about 130 b.h.p., and to help control its excesses the braking system had been uprated by installing 8″ diameter rear drums, and Mintex M171 front pads.

The car was able to accelerate to the benchmark 60 m.p.h. in a touch over eight seconds (in standard form it took about 8.6 seconds), and covered the standing quarter mile in only 16.0 seconds – almost three-quarters of a second better than a stock example. But what was most impressive about the car was its flexibility; tickover was a bit lumpy and there wasn't much to feel below 1800 r.p.m., but beyond there the power delivered very nicely indeed. The revised rear end enabled bends to be taken in a quite brisk manner, and the positive front end location reduced torque steer to a controllable level. I did, however, feel that in the damp the car could become something of a liability. Steering in the straight-ahead position was a little dead, and there was a tendency for the car to hook onto the white line when pulling out to overtake or changing lanes, but on the bendy bits the car showed its heritage, feeding back to the driver a constant flow of information.

The only aspect of the car that didn't impress was its braking system; for all of its abilities to haul the car down from whatever speed without any undue weaving or bobbing, the pedal felt consistently soggy. This is a characteristic of the car, and not the particular example which I was driving, and was due to the fairly convoluted route which an application of pressure had to make from the pedal through to the servo and master cylinder, which were situated on the other side of the car from the driver's seat. I believe that left-hand drive examples were far better in this respect, but that is no consolation to owners of British-market cars.

On balance, the car was worthy of the cult status that developed around it when it was available, and has since proven its right to appear on the growing roster of Ford greats. ●

RS TURBO

Fit a turbo and watch it go!

DENNIS FOY

The Escort RS Turbo marked something of a milestone in Ford of Britain's marketing strategy. For a start, it was the first car to come from the factory with a full RS bodykit already fitted to its panelwork. Then there was the fact that you could have the car in any colour you liked — so long as it was white. But the biggest departure from previous practice was that it was the first European production Ford to be fitted with a turbocharger system; up until that point, Ford's Special Vehicle Engineering (and its predecessor, Advanced Vehicle Operations) had favoured naturally-aspirated twin-cam engines from Lotus, and later Cosworth, to provide the motive power of their hottest models.

The car came into being as a successor to the Escort RS 1600i, and was intended to keep Ford ahead on the racetracks of Europe until such time as the all-new Sierra RS Cosworth was ready. Both cars had been conceived at the same product planning meeting at Ford of Britain's headquarters in early 1983, but as the Sierra RS project would involve a substantial amount of re-engineering, that car would not be ready to roll for some time. As the Escort would be a far-less-complex evolution of a current

RS car it could be in production far more quickly, and in fact went on sale to the public in September 1984, a full year ahead of its bigger brother. The RS Turbo served its purpose well, and notched up a string of successes throughout the 1985 racing season.

When the car first appeared, there were a few derisory comments — Ford are being "trendy" going turbo, and the like — but these were soon dispelled once examples of the car were available to test-drive. The car was built to race within the confines of Group A, which is the reason for the bodykit coming as standard — the car had to be able to accommodate a set of wheels some two or three inches wider than its road-wear when out on the circuit. For the same reason, the chosen turbocharger was a Garrett AiResearch T3 — it would have been more normal to fit a smaller T2 unit for road use on an engine of this size.

Another part of the RS Turbo's standard equipment which was decided on for racing purposes — but which has also been of great benefit to road car users — was the limited-slip differential, which ensures that drive is evenly distributed between the road ▶

RS TURBO

◄ wheels, even when traction is broken on one of them. The chosen unit was a fluid coupling, rather than the more common mechanical LSD systems of the day. This was developed by FF Developments, whose main claim to fame previously had been in developing the four-wheel drive system of the Jensen FF Interceptor. Even though the FF system is far "softer" than mechanical forms of LSD, those early examples of RS Turbo suffered quite severely from wheel tug through the steering. Not for nothing was the device nicknamed "vicious coupling".

The base for the car was the same bodyshell as that of the XR3i Escort, with no particular changes to its structure for the turbocharger. A minor contradiction of this car was the way in which it used the same rear spoiler as the XR3i, rather than that of the RS 1600i – despite Ford's 1982 claims that the German designed spoiler of the latter car was capable of developing greater downforce, and offering higher lateral stability at high speeds when compared with the XR3i piece. The RS bodykit, an Orion three-bar front grille, and extensive colour coding completed the bodywork specification of the Turbo model.

Mechanically, the tour is best commenced beneath the bonnet. A 1597cc Ford CVH engine was used, fitted with a set of low-compression pistons featuring improved ring design, uprated bearings, and revised gudgeon pins. To this was bolted a standard 1600 cylinder head casting equipped with sodium-filled exhaust valves, an Escort 1300 camshaft (its timing is particularly suitable to turbocharging, especially when

compared with the camshafts used in the XR3i and RS 1600i), and hydraulic cam followers.

Much of the credit for the turbocharger installation goes to Geoff Kershaw, head of Turbo Technics, who had worked closely with Ford's engineers during 1983 and 1984 whilst they put a number of turbocharged Escorts into competition to evaluate their worth. Such componentry as the exhaust manifold, a casting in high-nickel iron, was immediately identifiable as his handiwork. The T3 turbo blew through an intercooler adjacent to the radiator at the front of the car, and the cooled, compressed air was then ducted to the inlet plenum. Fuel was mixed in immediately before the charge entered the cylinders, and the chore of metering it was taken care of by a Bosch KE-Jetronic injection system. This worked in conjunction with a Bosch-Motorola engine management system which monitored, via sensors and its own circuitry, engine load, boost level, engine speed, and engine temperature at various points. As a safeguard there was a maximum engine speed cutout device incorporated which was supposed to "soft cut" the ignition and fuel systems as the redline was reached. However, in practice the device was extremely sudden in its operation.

As the engine was destined for a life on the racetrack, much work needed to be done to the transmission – partly for extra strength, and partly to accommodate the viscous coupling final drive arrangement. Accordingly, a new, heavy-duty casing was developed, along with a slightly revised final drive ratio and stronger gear teeth – these moves apparently overcoming a propensity of early prototypes to destroy their transmissions.

The suspension of the Mk I car was carried straight over from that of the RS 1600i, and made use of a cast-alloy front crossmember which allowed racers to alter the suspension geometry. MacPherson struts and a hefty anti-roll bar completed the front end arrangement. Unlike lesser Escorts, the RS package uses tie-bars to provide fore/aft location for the front struts, leaving the anti-roll bar free to be simply a spring assister; on most Escorts the bar fulfills both springing and location functions, which leads to problems with torque steer when a

powerful engine is employed. At the rear of the car, the familiar Escort swinging arm/coil spring/separate damper arrangement was augmented by a 12mm anti-roll bar from the Orion. This radically improved rear-end stability of the car, making it even better than that of the RS 1600i from which it evolved. Spring rates at either end of the car were the same as those found on the 1983-on XR3i. Girling dampers were standard issue, but a number of owners have found that their car's fast road behaviour has improved when they have replaced them with Bilstein items.

Bringing the car to a halt was the same braking system as that found on lesser models of Escort, notably the XR3i – although AP Racing discs on all four corners were homologated by Ford for their competition users, ordinary road-going mortals were lumbered with a disc/drum set-up on their cars. Improvement is a simple process, fortunately; a set of anti-fade pads and shoes, together with braided stainless steel hoses and race-quality fluid endows a standard car with far more suitable braking action for a car capable of almost 130 m.p.h. In contrast with the brakes, the wheel and tyre combination of the RS Turbo was very good, being 15" x 6" seven-spoke alloys with 195/50VR 15 tyres.

The Mk I RS Turbo was a superb car to drive. The engine delivered 132 brake horsepower, and was able to put a sizeable chunk of it down onto the tarmac thanks to the viscous coupling. The grey-trimmed Recaro seats were as effective as they were handsome, keeping both drivers and front passenger into place even under the most extreme cornering forces. The driver was presented with a standard XR3i fascia arrangement, complete with a soft-feel grey moulded steering wheel. Through the thick rim of that wheel the driver could tell what was going on at ground level at the front of the car, in time-honoured RS tradition – although the choice of tyres can affect the precise amount of response that makes its way back to the steering wheel.

I do, however, recall one trait of the car that was less than favourable, and that was the suddenness with which the rev-limited would come into play, all but shutting the engine down.

In a straight line this could be an uncomfortable experience, as the car would suddenly jolt. On a bend, it could be downright dangerous as all drive suddenly disappeared from the front wheels, totally upsetting the handling balance of the car. It also didn't do a lot for engine bearing life.

That apart, the car was exhilarating to use quickly. It took a few miles of fast bends to develop a "compensating factor" for the steering tug, but once that had been mastered it was possible to run the car very quickly, even on tight and twisting roads. Some of my colleagues expressed concern at the lack of bite from the brakes on their test examples of the car, but I could find no such problems with the example I was running — my only reservation was that the front wheels could be locked up quite easily if making a high-speed braking action in damp weather. Poor weather traction was otherwise excellent, thanks to the combination of Michelin MXV tyres and the viscous coupling.

The car was no slouch, either, despite its very limited turbo boost setting (whilst the design parameters were 3.5 to 7.5 lbs of boost, most cars were actually leaving the factory in Saarlouis with only four pounds of boost maximum), and was capable of seeing off most of its competition. I managed the benchmark 0-60 sprint in "my" test car in only 8.2 seconds, and the car subsequently went on to a maximum speed of 125 m.p.h. There was very little "lag" from the engine — although to get the best from the car it was advisable to keep the revs above 3000 when running hard in the countryside — and this accounted for the very good mid-gear times; 30-50 in fourth could be achieved in only seven seconds, and it took exactly the same time to achieve the 50-70 run in the same gear.

In all, some 5,500 examples of the car made their way into Britain, and a surprising number appear to have survived, despite close attention paid to them by car thieves. Prices are at present stable at about £6,000 for a good example, with perhaps forty thousand miles on the clock — lower mileage examples tend to command a slightly higher price, as might be expected, and the same goes for cars which were factory-fitted with the Custom Pack of sunroof, central locking, power windows, and tinted ▶

RS TURBO

glass. When buying, the areas to scrutinise closely are the turbocharger unit, which can show advanced signs of wear by 35,000 to 40,000 miles, the exhaust manifold, which can develop hairline cracks (which saps power), and the dampers, which again have a working life of about 30,000 miles or so. As with any car bearing a decent pedigree, try and find one which has a full service history, and bills for any components which have been replaced.

The last examples of the Mk I RS Turbo went on sale in early 1986, as the revisions being made to the Escort range would also include the RS Turbo model. By 1985 Ford's motorsport emphasis had shifted over to the awesomely-powerful RS Cosworth Sierra race and rally cars, and so it was no longer necessary to build the second model of RS Turbo with a whole range of in-built performance parts. In fact, the current, Mk II, Escort RS Turbo actually comes down the line at Saarlouis with the designation of XR3i Turbo, and is badged up as RS Turbo purely for the British market.

The car has the same engine format as previously, but with a revised management system which incorporated anti-knock circuitry, and with a lean-burn cylinder head. Power was still rated at the same 132 brake horsepower as that of the Mk I car, but the car feels distinctly flat when compared with the original model. Changes were also incorporated into the car's transmission, the overall gearing being raised in the interests of

improving the cruising noise levels of the engine by altering the final drive ratio from 4.27:1 to 3.82:1. A viscous coupling, now far less vicious in its action, is still fitted as standard to the car.

The suspension system of the car is fundamentally the same as that of the XR3i – gone are the separate tie bars of the front suspension, in their place being the 24mm anti-roll bar which has to double up its duties just like it does on all other Escorts. The front crossmember is now a steel pressing shared with other models within the range, meaning that there is no means of adjustment within the geometry of the car. At the rear, the RS Turbo still features an anti-roll bar, now a more substantial 16mm item.

The major gain that has been made over the early model of RS Turbo is the adoption as a standard feature of Ford's award-winning Stop Control System of anti-lock braking. Despite early misgivings over the all-mechanical system's worth (not on my part, I hasten to add), SCS has proven itself a valuable aid to safety.

What has been most upsetting to quite a few traditionalists is the appearance of the car. As there is no official competition interest in the car (the all-conquering Cosworth Sierras have become a full-time interest for Ford Motorsport), Ford found it unnecessary to equip the car with a radical bodykit which would enable wide slicks to be fitted to the car without upsetting its silhouette. In consequence, it can be difficult to tell the car apart from the less-powerful XR3i at first glance; only the twin bonnet louvres, subtle wheelarch trims and side skirtings set the current RS Turbo apart from its humbler kid brother.

The performance abilities of the car have become a contentious point, particularly in the area of the benchmark sprint from standstill to sixty. For example, we took our first test specimen of RS Turbo, a nice bright red one, down to the test track, and couldn't get to within a second of Ford's claimed time for the dash of 8.2 seconds. Yet a couple of weeks ago, we had the black model which graces these pages out, and managed a best time of 8.3 seconds. Our notes from the first test show that we had great difficulty in making the second-to-third upshift, which was where we were losing our time. With the newer car, we were able to make the upshift cleanly and with precision. All of our other times for the car were the same as our previous tests, give or take a couple of tenths here or there. In both cases, the maximum speed obtained was in the region of 125 miles per hour.

Out on the road, the car feels altogether softer than its predecessor, thanks principally to the revised settings of the viscous coupling (which tugs at the steering wheel a lot less than that of the Mk I car), and also to the lower specification of its suspension system. However, having said that, if the car is judged in its own right, rather than in the context of a comparison with the first Escort RS Turbo, it is fun to drive. It is quick enough and fast enough for most tastes, and providing the power level is left at its factory setting (rather than being "chipped" by the aftermarket), the handling is consistently safe and predictable – it is only when the horsepower figure rises beyond 140 or so that the suspension becomes woefully inadequate. If the lure of easy horsepower becomes too much for an owner to resist, a substantial amount of work needs to be done on the Mk II's suspension system to enable the chassis to cope. In counterpoint, the earlier car's abundance of racetrack-homologated parts enabled the standard car to take a power increase of up to thirty horsepower without any undue strain showing through on its underpinnings.

What the current model of car has become is often considered to be much less of an RS car than we have been used to – but Ford are well-known for following the dicta of the marketplace, so maybe nobody wants cars which tingle any more. Or maybe Ford have made an error of judgment ...?

●

RS 200

Group B rallying — outlawed too soon?

DENNIS FOY

The RS 1800 was a tough act to follow; that car, like the RS 1600 before it, had been stunningly successful on the international rallying scene, but the last rear wheel drive bodyshell went out of production in 1980 and so Ford had to look beyond the Mk II Escort and attempt to produce a car which would carry on the company's reputation in rallies with a more modern bodyshell. Ford Motorsport made a game attempt with the RS 1700T, a car which married the Mk III Escort bodyshell with technology derived from that of the Mk II car, but for reasons already detailed earlier in this series that car never achieved the required dual rôle of winning events and winning customer interest. When the new broom of Stuart Turner arrived as head of the company's International Motorsport Programme in 1983, one of his first moves was to abort the RS 1700T project, along with the C100 Endurance Racer programme.

Outsiders could have been forgiven for thinking that Ford had decided to quit whilst their motorsport reputation was still intact; observers of the rally scene were aware of the imminent threat from Audi, whose new Quattro was ready to come in and sweep the board. It would be perhaps more accurate to describe the retreat as a sabbatical — what Stuart Turner had in mind was a competition machine which would be much more than just a continuation of the previous cars and of the previous concept. What he had in mind was RS 200.

Just like every other field of international motorsport, rallying had its pecking order — and a car such as the 1700T would, in the mid '80s, be in Division One, and that meant it had to have four wheel drive, and immense amounts of power on instant call. The way that the groupings set by the Federation Internationale de l'Automobile worked at that time, the manufacturers needed to produce only two hundred examples of a car to ensure its eligibility for competition — and, as icing on the cake, they could then take ten percent of that production run and develop them further within the same basic format. Plans were rapidly put in hand to get the Ford name into Group B.

As Ford envisaged a worldwide benefit from having a car up there at the top of Division One, and as Ford products vary so much from nation to nation, it made no sense whatsoever to base the new competition car on an existing — or projected — production model. Additionally, the only four wheel drive cars which Ford had at that time were the Sierra and Granada

models, both of which were way too big and heavy to make the grade in Group B. A totally new chassis was designed by the eminent engineer John Wheeler, with input from Tony Southgate (now best-known for his excellent work with Jaguar's XJR endurance cars), and the details of this went out to Ford's Italian styling house Ghia of Turin.

There were quite a few differences of opinion between Ford Motorsport and Ghia concerning how the car ought to look — some of the early concept sketches were far too radical to ever become a practical rally car — but eventually, several arguments later, an acceptable design was agreed. Apparently the major stumbling block was the windscreen — Ford Motorsport wanted to use the screen of the Sierra, at a similar angle to that car's. Ghia, naturally, were more concerned with the overall styling of the car, and wanted to rake the front glass back quite sharply in the interests of a sleek appearance. Ford Motorsport won. ➤

RS 200

Meanwhile, John Wheeler was steadily refining his original chassis design. His overriding considerations were effectiveness and practicality, and the final design shows an inspired simplicity. The engine, a further development of the venerable Cosworth twin-cam BDT (Belt Driven, Turbocharged) was installed just ahead of the rear axle line, but back to front; the cam drive was rearmost. To the output end of the block was fitted a clutch housing and transfer box, which fed out the power forwards, via a short propshaft to the front transaxle. Both engine and transaxle were basically the same as those found in the aborted RS 1700T project; Ford are renowned for wasting nothing, especially in research and development time …

A longer, four-piece, propshaft then ran from front to rear axles of the car, supplying the back axle of the car with its portion of the power. It is a Ford philosophy of long standing that a slight rearwards bias is desirable in all-wheel drive cars, and so the power split of the RS 200 was determined at 37% to the front, and 63% to the rear. However, should circumstances dictate that a different split would enhance the car's chances of winning, it was possible to throw a short selector knob mounted adjacent to the gearlever and lock up the centre differential and divide the power equally between the two ends of the car. The same selector knob had a third setting, which would cancel out the front wheel drive and leave the car with all of its power going out through the rear wheels. Road cars did not have this option, owners being restricted to the 37/63 four wheel drive.

The simple beauty of John Wheeler's chassis meant that all four wheels were fed their power by equal-length halfshafts, which would minimise wear on the constant velocity joints — all four corners would have identical loads and stresses, which ought to ensure that there was no single weak spot. All three differentials within the driveline — one in each axle and one which divided power front front to rear — were equipped with FF viscous couplings, to ensure maximum traction at all times; viscous couplings are sophisticated slip limiters which use fluid viscosity as a means of controlling power feed.

Each corner of the car was independently sprung, with a pair of coil-over-damper units, one either side of the hub centreline. At the bottom of each hub location was taken care of by a wide-spaced tubular wishbone, and the steering was effected by the rack positioned just behind the front axle line. By having twin spring and damper units it was possible to vary the car's behaviour quickly and effectively; where necessary the car could be set up with just one spring at each corner, and the damper rates changed to suit conditions. Alternatively, the springing could be uprated to close on rock-solid. The essential beauty of the suspension system of the car was that whilst a tremendous amount of wheel travel was available, the attitude of each wheel and tyre to the road would remain constant regardless of how far up or down its twelve inches of potential travel it was. The entire system was so simple and versatile that it was possible to change the set-up of the car very quickly indeed — so quickly that a between-stages swap could be made during mixed-surface rallies.

The braking system was equally simple and effective, and entirely in keeping with the car's potential; a substantial 11.25" ventilated disc, an inch thick, was to be found outboard of each hub. On the front hubs a pair of AP Racing four-pot calipers were mounted on the leading edges, whilst at the rear two twin-pot calipers were fitted, one on the leading edge and the other on

"Once the necessary homologation papers had been signed some 46 of the 200 cars built were dissembled, to become a spares stockpile for future use."

the trailing edge of the disc. Such was the effectiveness of the system that a servo assister was considered superfluous, and so was not fitted. Outside of each disc was to be found a purpose-designed eight-spoke alloy wheel, sixteen inches in diameter and eight inches wide, shod with a Pirelli P700 tyre in a size of 225/50 x 16". For competition use, these were replaced by modular Speedline wheels of greater width still, shod with appropriately wider rubber — again generally supplied by Pirelli.

To power the car along, the BDT engine was revised and developed further from the state of tune it had been in when installed in the RS 1700T. The standard stroke of 77.62mm was retained, but the bore was taken out to 85.4mm, which gave an overall displacement of 1803cc. The engine sat at an angle of 23° from the vertical, the turbocharger side being uppermost, and the intake manifold was redesigned to suit the increased heat experienced by the engine being mounted amidships. The Ford EEC-IV engine management system was utilised in the RS 200, to control fuelling and ignition systems. The turbocharger itself was a Garrett unit, a hybrid of the T.03 and the T.04 — this gave the required amount of low-speed pulling power with adequate airflow at high engine speeds. In standard road trim the engine was set up to produce in the region of 235 brake horsepower, but close to double that would eventually become available for competition vehicles.

Although Ford Motorsport had been able to continue developing the car throughout 1983, final approval for the project still had to be gained from the main board of directors. Working from a chassis and a set of the final concept sketches, TC Prototypes (AFT) in Northampton produced a rolling example of RS 200 for evaluation by the board — and for that read the board of Ford World Headquarters, not just Ford of Britain, or even Ford Europe.

Fortunately for all involved, the massive amount of effort which had already gone into the project was rewarded by a concensus of approval. RS 200 was given the green light.

During 1984 another half-dozen examples of the car were produced at Boreham, prior to the rest of the intended production run going ahead at Reliant's Shenstone factory near Coventry. There were a few changes made to the car during the prototype development period, mainly in the area of the bodyshell's various appendages; only when the first bodyshell was put into a wind tunnel and its behaviour assessed could the effectiveness of such items as air intakes be accurately gauged, and altered to optimise their efficiency. One major change, however, came about by less scientific means, when car number four was on its way up to a sub-contractor's premises for evaluation.

The first cars had their rear body panel section rear-hinged, GT40-style, their leading edges being retained by a pair of over-centre panel clips. Unfortunately, somebody had on this particular day omitted to double-check that the clips were secured before the driver toddled off up the M1. The air intake

which is situated just above the roofline is attached to the rear panelwork and, yes, you've guessed it, the wind whipped the entire rear section open and tore it off the back of the car like it was made from wet tissue paper ...

That is why every example of RS 200 from number four onwards has the rear bodywork hinging the other way around, with the main fixing being to the rear of the cockpit roof.

RS 200 went into series production at Shenstone in 1985, the Reliant work force being joined by a number of Ford's own people on secondment from Boreham. Reliant were chosen for several reasons, the principle one of which was their expertise with laminates, not just glassfibre reinforced plastics but also such materials as Ararmid, Kevlar, and carbon fibre. The RS 200 was designed from the outset as a monocoque central hub with fore and aft sub-chassis, the central section being made around honeycomb alloy laminated with a variety of man-made materials. The combination gave the required package of extremely high strength with a minimum of weight. On the outer sections of the central tub steel panels were bonded into place, in the interests of impact durability; Stuart Turner was

understandably obsessive on matters of safety, and the inclusion of these panels was very much a safety matter. The doors were derived from the Sierra (it was the adoption of Sierra doors which pre-determined the angle of the windscreen, and thus ensured that Ghia couldn't stray too far from their original brief), but by the time that they made made it onto RS 200 they were not recognisable as such; the composite mouldings shared a few vital dimenions with their parent, but that was about all. The nose and tail sections of production models were principally made from glassfibre-reinforced plastics, augmented by carbon fibre around their mounting points.

In order to satisfy the FIA inspectorate, Ford made available for inspection a total of two hundred cars, including the pre-production examples. However, once the appropriate homologation papers had been signed, some forty six of the built cars were dissembled, to become a spares stockpile for future use; after all, what was the sense in having a vast stock of completed cars standing around unsold — especially when another car could be conjured up out of the "spares" if and when required?

Ford's choice of Reliant to produce the main run of cars was a wise one, if the appearance of the finished cars is anything to go by; the strength, integrity and smoothness of panel of the Shenstone-built cars is beyond reproach.

Meanwhile the car's rally testing programme was going on with a vengeance. In addition to much track-testing with none other than Jackie Stewart at the wheel, other examples from the original prototype run of cars were to be found on rally courses and off-highway tracks throughout Europe, being put through their paces with such drivers as Malcolm Wilson at the helm. Power outputs varied, with as much as 425 brake horsepower being available — although interestingly the EEC-1V management system was not used on the competition versions of the engine, due to a lack of development time. Instead, a Motronic unit controlled the vital functions of fuel and sparking. The overall concensus was that the car was a potential ➤

RS 200

winner — and sure enough, first time out with Malcolm Wilson and Nigel Harris occupying the cosy cabin on the 1985 Lindisfarne Rally, the RS 200 scored a resounding victory.

A second success came the RS 200's way a few months later, in January 1986, when long-time Ford star driver Stig Blomqvist piloted the car to second place in the Norway national rally. Both of those events, incidentally, were entered prior to the car gaining its homologation papers, which only came through on February 1st 1986. Following the car's acceptance in Group B, Ford campaigned the RS 200 vigorously with mixed degrees of success; wins in the Ardennes, Centro and Tulip rallies were countered by a string of retirements and low placings in other events during the spring of '86. Fortunately, the act did come good, and the car was able to claim a total of nineteen international wins with a further thirteen placings in the top three.

Interestingly, all of the successes came with the car in its standard trim, rather than in Evolution form. This again was attributable to the hand of Stuart Turner, who held strong views on the subject of Evolution cars; basically his prime interest was in winning with the car as designed, rather than what it might be evolved into.

There was an increasing feeling of unease throughout the rally world concerning Group B, the general opinion being that the cars of Audi, Austin Rover, Ford, Lancia and Peugeot were basically too fast and too powerful to be safe. A string of

accidents confirmed these fears as being founded — first Joachim Santos crashed into a solid wall of spectators on the Portuguese Rally, killing three, then Kalle Grundel seriously injured a young boy on the Circuit of Ireland when his car caught him on a bend. What didn't aid Ford's management was that both incidents involved RS 200s. More tragedy was yet to come for Group B. During May 1986 the much-respected and vastly-experienced team of Henri Toivonen and Sergio Cresto crashed their Lancia S4 — killing both men. Shortly after the Toivonen crash the F.I.S.A. met, and decided that the remainder of the year's events would be shortened to the minimum acceptable duration, and that from 1987 onwards the World Series of rallies would be for Group A, rather than Group B cars. This meant that a minimum of 5,000 examples of a car would have to be built before homologation would be granted — effectively outlawing the RS 200, 6R4, Audi, Lancia S4 and Peugeot Group B cars.

The RS 200 programme had cost Ford a considerable amount of money — anything up to £12.5 million once the final sums had been worked out — and they could have found themselves with an expensive headache, being lumbered with almost a hundred and fifty high-powered rally cars with no rallies to run them in. Fortunately, a decision had been taken very early on in the programme to submit the standard RS 200 for full Type Approval, which would enable Ford to sell as many examples as they could for road use. This had been an expensive proposition — including the crash testing of a complete car — but it was proved a worthwhile venture once the car had been outlawed for competition use.

Given the amount of cash pumped into the RS 200 programme by Ford's international management, it is unsurprising to learn that the asking price for the road-going version of the car started at a cool fifty thousand pounds. For that the buyer got a pure RS car just one step removed from the competition machine. To make the car acceptably civilised it was necessary to completely strip down every example set aside for sale, and to then rebuild

The BDT engine is mounted amidships, with the block at an angle of 23° from the vertical to allow the main driveshaft to pass along the centre of the car.

it; the original cars had been assembled just enough to pass muster, the principal being that owners intending to use the car for competition purposes would tear the car down and build it up to their specification anyway.

The car as originally assembled was noisy, suffered from driveline vibrations making their way into the cockpit — and was also very harsh-riding. Once the decision to sell a hundred and twenty road examples had been taken, these problems needed to be attended to. Whilst the suspension rates were left basically unchanged from the road rates set early on in the programme, the bushings originally employed were considered too harsh and so softer items were installed throughout the car. Strategic soundproofing pads were installed within the car's cabin as the rebuild progressed, pads which would subsequently be hidden by the mid-grey velour carpeting used throughout the cabin's lower section. Ford had experienced a problem with electronic interference during the life of the car — and not the expected radio supression problems, but interference with the signals received on nearby television sets whenever an RS 200 was in the vicinity. To overcome this a large black moulded box was

"It is only when the throttle is stabbed with real gusto on the apex of a bend that the rearwards bias of the car's driveline makes itself known ..."

designed and made, and then fitted atop the Cosworth engine. This effectively baffled the engine management system, which was the root cause of the problem.

The occupants of the car were offered a choice of either red or black Sparco lightweight bucket seats in which to sit, seats which were shape-hugging but extremely comfortable and supportive. There was also the option of leather trim, should the purchaser wish to have that particular finish. Facing the driver was a neatly-designed binnacle containing a speedometer to the right and an oil pressure gauge to the left — with a teaplate-sized tachometer slap-bang in the middle. The steering column head assembly, complete with switchgear and wheel, would be familiar territory to any Mk III Escort owner, as it was taken straight from that car — whilst the rocker switches which ranged across the centre of the fascia came from the Fiesta. Above the switches were four further round gauges which monitored the remaining vital functions of the car. All that the passenger got was a bin for stowing odds and sods.

Being designed as a purely functional competition machine, the RS 200 was not exactly endowed with masses of stowage space. Apart from the little bin ahead of the passenger there was a vestigal "luggage box" mounted in the nose of the car, and that was it. The basic attitude to adopt, should you ever be fortunate enough to own one of these machines, is that if it won't go into a small, squashy overnight bag then you don't take it with you. Other facets of the car which gave away its origins as a rally car were such details as the total absence of any kind of stereo system as standard (although Ford were magnanimous enough to provide a DIN-sized fascia aperture ready to accept a radio-cassette unit) and the manual window winders.

But then, to criticise the car for such details would be quite unfair, churlish even. The RS 200 was conceived as a competition vehicle and the road cars which came about as a result of the FIA's rule changes were, as I mentioned earlier, pretty damned close in their behaviour. In fact the car is so close to being a full-house rally machine that it was available only

direct from Ford; dealerships only ever got their hands on one of the two or three rally cars which were seconded out to the promotions department once their working lives were over. Basically, anybody wanting to purchase an example of RS 200 was handed over to Bob Howe, the former head of product planning at Ford Advanced Vehicle Operations, who having officially retired from Ford had been tempted back on a consultancy basis to look after the RS 200 sales and marketing strategy.

Bob, an affable character whose energy and enthusiasm belie the fact that he has exceeded the corporate retiring age, would ten offer a fully-illustrated presentation on RS 200 before taking the potential client out onto the Boreham test track and introducing him or her to the sheer exciting reality of the car.

The driver doesn't so much sit in RS 200 as wear it, so snugly do the controls fit the driver's physique. The example which I drove was number two hundred, the very last off the line, a car which is set up for driving in places other than Britain — hence its left hand drive controls. The supportive seat isn't too easy to get into or out of, but once there is comfortable and highly effective at keeping the occupant in place regardless of cornering speed. Firing up the BDT — which in this particular car produces in the region of 250 b.h.p. — and keeping the revs below 1500 r.p.m. for the first few moments as instructed, I was able to ascertain immediately that whilst much work has gone into producing a road car which is far more civilised than the competition versions of the car, it is still some way off having the smoothness of any regular production car; it sizzles and buzzes just like a GT40.

In the same way as the Forty, the RS 200 settled down quite soon to a smoother and more acceptable tickover — time, thought I, to see what the car feels like out on Boreham's sweeping curves. ►

The bodyshell was designed by Ghia — with restrictions imposed by Ford Boreham regarding screen shape and position. It is hard to see now, but doors were basically Sierra items, to suit windscreen!

RS 200

The car has become a legend within its own lifetime amongst those members of the motoring press fortunate enough to try one as being impossible to pull away smoothly in for the first time; almost without exception my colleagues stalled the car. Still smarting from a similar experience with John Wooler's immaculate RS 1800 recently — the first time that I had stalled a car in years, or so my memory would have me believe — I was determined to break the 200's duck and make a clean virgin getaway. I didn't. The sharpness and suddenness of the 7.3" twin-plate AP Racing clutch got me and I too joined the long list of motoring scribes who have stalled RS 200.

I got it right the second time though, and set off for a couple of exploratory laps of the track; I was in a car I didn't know, on a track I hadn't driven in some years. This was no time for heroics. And anyway, Bob Howe was sitting quietly in the passenger seat, and he knows far more about driving two hundreds quickly than I could ever pick up in a couple of hours whopping around Boreham — even if it had been in my nature to try and impress him, I doubt whether I could.

The car's weight balance is split almost perfectly, with 48% to the front and 52% to the rear, and this matches nicely with the power division of the four-wheel drive system. Even at speeds which would have most cars spinning off towards the outfield of Boreham's bends the car remains pleasingly neutral; it is only when the throttle is stabbed with real gusto on the apex of a bend that the rearwards bias of the drive makes itself known, pushing the tail of the car out lightly and controllably. The engine spins readily towards its redline (set at seven thousand for the road car, but obviously higher on competition machines), and the power delivers smoothly and immediately. There is no sensation of turbo lag with this car, merely a turbine-smooth, solid wave of muscle making its way through the driveline.

Number two hundred had been stood for a little while, and the clutch mechanism wasn't quite as smooth as it might be thanks to a sticking release bearing, but even so the car was surprisingly easy to drive smoothly and cleanly once rolling. The weighting of the clutch pedal is heavy, as befits a twin-plate assembly, but this is only a problem when driving in traffic; out on the run the pressure is not noticeably excessive. Much the same can be said of the steering action, which is as heavy as might be expected at low speeds (thanks to the 225/50 tyres), but which becomes pleasingly lighter as higher speeds are attained. The feedback to the driver is exactly as it ought to be, with all four wheels declaring their intentions before they do anything untoward.

Given the tremendous amount of travel built into the suspension system of the car, I had expected the car to roll on corners and curves far more than it actually does; even at very high cornering speeds the RS 200 maintains a flat attitude — and is able to deal with imperfections in the road surface with aplomb. As so often happens with ultra high-performance cars, the RS 200's ride quality is appreciably better at high speed than it is when pottering along slowly, the car soaking up the bumps with no difficulty whatsoever.

As might be expected from the specification, the car's braking system is highly effective, if heavy on the right foot; retardation is immediate and in direct proportion to the amount of pressure applied to the middle pedal, with the car displaying no tendencies to weaving or bobbing even under hard braking. My speeds around Boreham's circuit had progressively increased as my senses grew familiar with the car, and I was eventually turning in laps which were quicker than I had ever intended — or expected. All credit for this goes to the car, which is capable of making stunningly quick progress around the track. What was particularly impressive about the car was the way in which it was so untiring; I got out, after driving the equivalent distance to a run from Manchester to Birmingham, on a reasonably demanding track, feeling quite fresh.

The rear panels of the first few cars were rear-hinged, GT40-style. Only when one blew off the car was the arrangement changed to front-edge hinging.

The car never lets the driver forget its heritage, though, for all of its relative sophistication. For instance, the gearshift mechanism runs on Rose joints, and in consequence has a variety of "zizzing" noises in its repertoire, depending on the gear selected. The action of the shift mechanism is solid, and a positive hand is called for at all times if missed shifts are to be avoided. Then there is the visibility. Looking out through the front screen and the side glass is fine, no worse than any other model in the current Ford line-up, but rear visibility is virtually non-existent, thanks to the tinted rear engine cover. Out on the run it is advisable to forget all about using the interior rear view mirror, and instead use the dor-mounted items, just like you would in a van.

In standard form the RS 200 is a stimulating, exciting car to drive. In Evolution specification it must be close to mind-blowing.

Despite the fact that the rules were changed before the 20 Evolution models were given the opportunity to compete, Boreham went ahead and built some anyway, at the request of specific customers. There is more to that particular car than just a change of microchip and a bit of reprogramming to increase the power output to the expected 600 b.h.p. For a start, the normal RS 200 engine, which was built up by J.Q.F. to run at anything from eleven to eighteen pounds of boost, was unable to deliver the required extra musclepower, despite its full-race complement of internal components. Instead, a Brian Hart-developed bigger block (referred to as the BDT/E) which was some 20mm longer than the standard item was installed, the extra length being necessary to allow an overbore which would take displacement out to 2137cc. When equipped with a larger turbocharger, greater intercooler, additional fuel rail and lower compression pistons the engine could be boosted with up to 25 lbs of turbo pressure — enough to give the desired six hundred horses.

Much of the chassis could remain as was, thanks to the considerable amount of expertise which had gone into it initially, but the clutch and transmission were uprated to handle the power increase. Finally, the body panels were moulded in a lighter laminate than the normal GRP, saving anything up to 120 lbs. Nobody has been prepared to attach a price tag to the Evolution model — suffice to say it is appreciably more expensive than the standard car.

Of the RS 200s which have been sold by Ford (all offered have now gone, although a number have yet to be delivered), the biggest proportion have stayed in Britain — some 52 cars are still within our islands. 27 have gone out to the U.S.A., with a further 20 going north of the border into Canada. The Japanese have bought 14 (it is unknown whether they will be producing a copy in a couple of years' time ...), and there are seven in Sweden, six in West Germany, and four each in Spain and Norway. Finland, Indonesia and Switzerland have a couple each, and there is one each in France, Italy, Monaco, Luxembourg and Portugal.

What the future holds in store for the RS 200 is uncertain. The chances are very, very high that it will be viewed as a classic with its value rising accordingly. Given the strictly limited availability of the car, some parallel between this car and such machinery as the Ferrari F40, the Porsche 959 and the Aston Martin Vantage Zagato is inevitable — but may not necessarily be fair. For a start, those three cars were conceived as all-out road cars, even if all three have totally different approaches to the issue. For instance, whilst the F40 is as close as you can get to a road-legal Ferrari racer, the chances of seeing one of these cars being used on a track in serious competition are slim. The Aston was conceived as a special-bodied version of the existing Vantage with a more

powerful engine, but no aspirations towards motorsport in any form. And the 959 was put out by Porsche to prove just how far the Stuttgart company could push forward the barriers of automotive technology.

The RS 200 is none of these things. It was created as a rally car, and when the rules were changed quite a high proportion of the run was offered for sale in road trim. In that sense a fairer comparison would be to Ford's own GT40 — and in character, too, the 200 is closer to the Forty than it is to the Aston, the Ferrari or the Porsche.

The eventual value of the individual RS 200 will, in future years, be at least partially governed by its authenticity. It is likely that one of the Strattons of Wilmslow leather-trimmed versions will command a slightly higher value than would one which had been built up to standard specification by Tickford. However, having said that, I can foresee some real ding-dong battles going on with "experts" in the future concerning the trim and equipment built into any particular example of the car: "This should have red Sparcos not grey Recaros ..." and so forth. However, because of the "bespoke" service offered by Bob Howe and his team at Boreham virtually any trim package which would fit within the narrow confines of the car's cockpit could be had. And there is at least one example of RS 200 with Escort RS Turbo-style Recaros fitted within the cabin.

The final area of authenticity concerns the colour of the car. In typical Ford Boreham style, the RS 200 was available in any colour you liked, as long as it was Diamond White. However, a number of owners expressed a desire to have the car in an alternative shade — presumably because the white ones are frightfully common. There are subsequently at least four red RS 200s in existence, and one black one. More colours are bound to follow before the end of June 1989 when the final car is scheduled to be handed over to its purchaser. ●

DANCING
on
TIPTOES

FULL TEST: THE SIERRA RS500 COSWORTH

DENNIS FOY

With my hand on my heart, I can honestly say that I consider this to be the best car that Ford have ever produced. With acceleration to sixty from standstill taking less than six seconds, and a maximum speed on the far side of 150 m.p.h., it isn't quite the fastest car that the corporation have ever produced; those honours must surely go to the legendary GT40 which could, in road trim, manage perhaps 175 m.p.h. whilst achieving the sprint to sixty in perhaps five seconds.

However, for all of the spiritual ties that exist between these two cars (both were conceived as race machines, with de-tuned versions being available for road use), they are very different animals. No matter how much mystique has been built up over the years, the fact remains that the GT40 is essentially noisy, cramped, uncomfortable, and generally short on creature comforts. The RS500, on the other hand, is quiet, spacious, comfortable, and well-equipped.

Anybody who has ever driven an original GT40 over any sort of distance on the roads will agree that the car could never be described as pleasant to drive: appointments to have an osteopath correct the spinal jarring, a dentist to refit the shaken-loose fillings and a doctor to cure the heatstroke ought to be made at the other end of any lengthy journey. I reckon that anybody who has taken one of these cars more than a couple of hundred miles on A-roads should automatically qualify for a Duke of Edinburgh Endurance Scheme Award.

Conversely, anybody can get into a Cosworth RS500, drive it from one end of the country to the other, and emerge feeling fresh and untired. This car brings a new depth to the description Grand Tourer, as it really is perfect for touring in the grand manner.

DANCING
on
TIPTOES

◁ When the original Cosworth Sierra appeared on the scene last year, it was immediately successful as a racing car. However, it could have been more successful, had there been one or two changes made. Ford have capitalised on the Group A Racing rule which allows 10% of a homologated car's production run to be further developed as "evolution" cars, with improved performance. Hence the appearance of the RS500.

The engine of the RS500 is substantially altered from the standard Cosworth unit. The block has been substantially strengthened by the reduction of sand cores within the casting, which leads to a thicker wall section between cylinders, and an increase in strength to the top and bottom decks. This should effectively cancel any tendency to twisting by the block whilst hot. The move should also bring about an end to the problem of blown head gaskets on the engine, which has sidelined one or two racers during the course of the car's first season on the track.

The pistons of the RS500 are also uprated, and there is an uprated spray bar which aims jets of cooling oil to their

Ford have taken their already-impressive Cosworth, and treated it to a package of high-performance engine parts. In doing so, they have made a great car close to perfect.

undersides. An uprated oil pump is provided on the RS500 engine to ensure that this is kept supplied.

It is, however, the induction system which shows the greatest change on this engine when compared with the standard. A completely new turbocharger is installed, which is substantially larger than that of the basic car's T3 Garrett item. The new turbo is a hybrid, using half each of a Garrett T31 and T04 unit. This feeds from a cast 4/2/1 exhaust manifold, and surplus gases are dealt with by an integral wastegate. The inlet tract is increased in diameter by 16%, and the plenum is similarly larger to cope with the increased airflow from the larger turbocharger. A new full-width air-to-air intercooler is installed, which reduces the temperature of the incoming charge to 45°C, which makes for an improvement in air density as it enters the engine – thus improving the engine's efficiency. For the 500, the engine is fitted with a secondary fuel rail and injector set which is not active on the road cars – but can be brought into play by hooking them up, and by replacing the Electronic Control Unit (E.C.U.) which masterminds the engine's electrical and fuel systems.
And therein lies the key to the future success of the RS500 as a racing machine, for by replacing the E.C.U. with a new unit, the turbocharger wastegate pressure can be altered, along with the ignition timing and fuel feed systems, to immediately push the power output from the standard 224 b.h.p. to something in the region of four hundred horsepower – or anything in between the two. And the cost of such a move would be in the hundreds, rather than thousands of pounds, mark. What the customer is getting for the £3,000-ish premium in price asked for the RS500 is a degree of over-engineering that will allow the power to be uprated to whatever level the race team feels appropriate for the specific race or circuit, without any harmful effect on the engine itself.

On certain circuits with lots of bends and short straights, the original Cosworth has shown a tendency for the brakes to get excessively hot – leading, on occasion, to the fluid boiling up, and a marked reduction in efficiency. If Ford had ducted air from the intakes on the front spoiler of the original car to the brake rotors this problem would have been less severe, but they didn't, and the M.S.A. won't allow such ducting on race cars, so what Ford have done on the RS500 is to do away with the auxilliary driving lamps that are found inboard of the trafficators of the standard Cosworth, leaving a pair of grilled vents in their place. This ought to allow the necessary additional cooling air to the front hubs, and thus bring an end to the problem.

"Replacing the Electronic Control Unit will put the power up to 400 b.h.p."

During our week with the car we did our usual stint of seeking valid opinions from various parties, and in the case of the RS500 this involved having a couple of people who run standard Cosworths try out the newcomer, and tell us how they feel it compares. Racer Tim Harvey was one such person, as in addition to racing the machines, he also runs one as daily transport. His initial reaction was one of disappointment, as he felt that the car was slower than his own model is – until a glance at the speedometer showed that his progress was, in fact, more rapid than he considered it to be. On Tim's car, as with any standard-specification Cosworth, there is a marked surge in power when the turbocharger comes onto boost which heightens the senses, and relates instantly to fast driving. With the revised turbocharger of the RS500 the torque spread of the car is substantially broader, and the onset of positive boost is far less pronounced. In practice, the car doesn't actually feel like a turbocharged machine – it merely feels like it has a turbine under the bonnet which keeps feeding in more and more power.

My first encounter with the RS500 was on a wet Friday morning, here in Cheshire. The inside of the car is identical to that of the standard Cosworth, and is thus not dissimilar to any Sierra. Adjusting the Recaro seat so that I was perfectly positioned in relation to the controls was a simple process (the seat can be adjusted for height as well as reach and rake, and the knee support can also be altered), and in within a moment or two of first entering the car I fired up the engine, and rumbled out of the car park of the Four Seasons, the hotel which Ford had selected as the base for the Press Testing Day. In view of the weather I decided against taking the car onto the motorway adjacent to the hotel, and instead headed off onto a route I had already driven along that morning in an RS Turbo Escort. This took in narrow, tight-winding country lanes, long sweeping A-roads, and a few testing variations in road surface. The Escort had dealt with the route neatly, never deviating from its intended line. Dry weather would have enabled more rapid progress, but I have always felt that there is no room in my world for fair-weather cars. Or at least not until we are a shade more affluent, and can afford the indulgence of a Morgan in the garage for sunny afternoons ...

And anyway, taking high-performance cars out in poor weather conditions highlights their vices early, at speeds where they ought not come to harm should something go wrong.

I was immediately impressed by the massive torque spread of the engine, which was quite happy to potter along in the local traffic at only a little above its tickover speed. The car took a few minutes to come up to temperature, and I found that it had a tendency towards brake grab until such point as the pads were properly warmed through; this went once the car was up to operating temperature, leaving a firm, prompt-acting, but progressive braking action. Turning off the main road and leaving the traffic behind, I rolled on some power — and immediately went sideways. The oh-so-sharp steering responded instantly and brought the car back into line, but it was a salutary warning that I would obviously have to treat this machine with kid gloves (or kid shoes, to be anatomically correct) if I was to return it to the hotel intact. With the Escort RST that I had been trying earlier, it had been possible to pile on the power once the line through a curve was established, correcting any understeer by playing the throttle. With the Cosworth RS500, a far more "pussyfooting" approach soon proved itself to be the rule of the day. When I finally returned to the Four Seasons I was of the opinion that the car was a handful

in the wet — but nevertheless relishing its appearance Chez Foy the following Tuesday morning, when it was scheduled to arrive for a week-long test. Monday night, I prayed for dry weather.

The weather was dry for most of the time that I spent with the car, and I discovered that it really is a delightful car to drive. Its straight-line performance is simply stunning — and unmatched by anything this side of fifty grand's worth of Italian or German exotica. But where the car really comes into its own is on the bends. There is an almost telepathic quality to the steering which enables the car to be pointed into, directed through, and exited from even the most vicious of bends without even having to consider a physical movement of the steering wheel. To feel that a car is an extension of the driver's body, and that the driver is an integral part of the machine, is a rare phenomenon — but one which most definitely applies to the RS500. The front wheel geometry of the car has been altered by Rod Mansfield's team at Ford, and this has endowed the car with a precision

which makes the standard Cosworth feel woolly by comparison. Combining this with the massive amounts of power that can be fed in with a progression unmatched by any other car I have ever driven and with a transmission that is faultless in its shifting quality, and the car adds up to a feeling that it has been put together like a Rolex watch.

Coming off a long straight onto a series of curves, a squeeze on the brakes is enough to scrub off as much speed as the oncoming bend merits. The light, progressive clutch and snickety-snick gearbox has the ratio changed before the driver even has to think about it, and the perfect spring rates and damping have the car dancing through the first curve on tiptoes. Once the exit of the curve is in sight the throttle can be applied to the necessary degree to sweep on for the next stretch of road. Repeating the procedure through as many curves as the road cares to make has the car simply eating them up and asking for more. With this car it is possible to sweep along at a velocity that would have had more mortal cars in the ditch at the roadside, without the slightest feeling of urgency, and with a reassuring constant feedback through the car to all of the driver's senses.

Big, fat Dunlop D4 tyres form the link between car and road surface, and as with every other component on the car these proved an ideal choice, enabling the car to be drifted gently, ever-controllably, into sweeping curves with just a hint of a song coming from the rubber. Then, when the end of the bend is in sight, the power can be squeezed on, the car tightens its line, the rubber bites as torque from the viscous-coupled rear axle evens out between both driven wheels, and the car simply rockets away from the bend. Onward, ever onward should be engraved on the dashboard of these cars.   ▷

DANCING *on* TIPTOES

◁ It is reassuring to know that, should an emergency arise, the braking system is equipped with the Alfred Teves anti-lock mechanism, which will enable very rapid, totally safe stops to be made. However, having said that, anybody who reaches the point of pushing a Cosworth RS500 to the point where they are getting into trouble cannot be paying attention to the many signals that make their way back to the driver from all points of the car; the machine positively tingles as it proceeds along the road. Until the Cosworth came along, power-assisted steering was a necessary evil, where the choices were either to have light and manoeuvrable steering with a dead, feel-less point in the straight-ahead position, or there was feel at all points of the steering radius, with superhuman effort required at parking speeds. The steering of this car, however, is an object lesson in

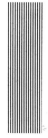

"Unmatched by anything this side of fifty grand's worth of Italian or German exotica."

getting it right; effort is lightly-weighted, feedback from the roadwheels is instant, and response is nothing short of perfect. For all of the car's mechanical perfection, I'm afraid that I would find it difficult to live with a couple of its facets; those damned spoilers. On the RS500 the rear spoiler has had a lip added to it, and this serves to reduce the already-poor rear visibility of the standard car still further — to the point where all that can now be seen of the following car is the blue light on its roof. At the front of the car there is another new addition, a rubber lip which attaches, in two parts, to the lower part of the one-piece front moulding. This is a pure racetrack part, as is the rear spoiler set-up, but is of little use on the road unless the car is going to spend much of its life on autobahns. With the strip in place, the ground clearance is reduced to something like 2" (about an inch

less than a standard Cosworth), with the result that even the slightest pothole in the road becomes a danger zone. I had been in possession of the car for exactly 24 hours when, approaching Oulton Park's main gate, I hit a pothole in the road which neatly removed the nearside half of the spoiler, snapping the plastic clips which retained it. Having been unable to obtain the necessary clips from our local dealers in time to complete the photo sessions booked with the car, I resorted to bolting the thing back on using electrical set-screws. I only hope that whoever tests the car next doesn't catch the spoiler extension, as I have the distinct feeling that they might end up ripping off the entire front moulding of the car!

Interestingly, by the time that the week of testing the car was coming to an end (during which time the car had done the usual thousand or so miles), I had mastered its initial wayward manners in wet weather. Yes, some degree of pussyfooting was still in order, but for the most part I found that what was needed was to treat the controls delicately — just as the car merited in the dry, but more so.

In terms of equipment and creature-comforts, the RS500 is up there in the big league. The Recaro seats are supremely comfortable, and it is possible to adjust them to suit drivers of virtually any height and size. Soundproofing is more than adequate, and the car is trimmed with deep-pile carpeting. A sunroof, power windows, central locking, high-grade, four speaker stereo, power-adjustable mirrors and so forth are all standard items, though the car is not equipped with the Chubb anti-theft locks that current models of Sierra have. One little detail touch that impressed me was the way in which the automatic radio aerial, mounted to the offside rear wing, retracted itself every time that the bootlid lock was depressed — this meant that the danger of catching the mast whilst loading the boot was minimised. As soon as the tailgate was slammed shut the aerial went up again. Neat.

SPECIFICATIONS
FORD SIERRA RS500 COSWORTH

ENGINE TYPE	4 cylinder DOHC	BRAKING SYSTEM	Teves anti-lock, all disc, servo assisted
BORE x STROKE	90.8mm x 77mm		
SIZE	1993cc	WEIGHT	2734 lbs
BHP @ RPM	224 @ 6000	POWER/WEIGHT RATIO	186 b.h.p./ton
TORQUE LB/FT @ RPM	280 @ 4500	WHEELBASE	102.7"
FUEL SYSTEM	Weber Marelli electronic injection, Garrett T31/T03 Turbocharger	LENGTH	176"
		HEIGHT	54"
TRANSMISSION	5 speed manual	WIDTH	75"
DRIVEN WHEELS	Rear	TEST MILEAGE	1,063 miles
SUSPENSION: FRONT	McPherson struts with anti-roll bar	TEST MPG	17.0
		MANUFACTURER'S MPG	20.6
SUSPENSION: REAR	Independent, trailing arms with anti-roll bar	PRICE AS TESTED	£19,995
		INSURANCE GROUP	Special quotation

MANUFACTURER: Ford Motor Company, Dagenham, Essex, England.

MEETING THE OPPOSITION

Acceleration 0-60

SIERRA RS500 COSWORTH 5.9 secs	
BMW M5 6.2 secs	
BMW M635CSi 6.2 secs	
MERCEDES-BENZ 2.3-16 7.5 secs*	
PORSCHE 944 TURBO 6.3 secs*	
PORSCHE 911 CARRERA 6.1 secs*	

*To 62.5 m.p.h.

Maximum speeds

SIERRA RS500 COSWORTH 153 m.p.h.	
BMW M5 153 m.p.h.	
BMW M635CSi 158 m.p.h.	
MERCEDES-BENZ 2.3-16 143 m.p.h.	
PORSCHE 944 TURBO 152 m.p.h.	
PORSCHE 911 CARRERA 152 m.p.h.	

Prices

SIERRA RS500 COSWORTH £19,995	
BMW M5 £34,850	
BMW M635CSi £40,950	
MERCEDES-BENZ 2.3-16 £25,540	
PORSCHE 944 TURBO £36,080	
PORSCHE 911 CARRERA £35,576	

What did perplex me at first was the absence of a boost gauge from the otherwise-comprehensive instrument cluster. Then I realised that it did have one after all — but it was tucked away in the corner of the speedometer, perfectly concealed from line of sight by the leather-rimmed RS steering wheel.

When the original Cosworth appeared, its reception was virtually unanimous; almost everybody that came into contact with the car felt that it was a serious supercar, one which took on the might of Porsche, BMW and the like, and beat them. It would be difficult to even match that standard, but what Ford have done with the RS500 is to make a great car even greater. It is even better to drive — in some respects it is easier, and in no respects is it more difficult or less rewarding — and it has an in-built performance potential to enable the car to see off just about anthing else on the market. What is more, I cannot honestly see these cars depreciating in value. Of the five hundred that have been built, the majority are destined for life on the race tracks, which leaves only a small number to enjoy life on the roads. Anybody with the capital to be able to afford to buy one and store it for a couple of years will surely see a massive return on their investment.

However, even if I had the money to pursue such a move, I couldn't; such is the pleasure of driving this car, my heart wouldn't let me own one and not use it. I would be out there at the slightest opportunity, savouring the car's obvious delights. And if I wasn't, Pat would be. It is that kind of car. ●

ARRIVAL

Ford's four-door RS Cosworth has finally arrived. Ian Corry has been to Sicily to sample the newcomer's delights. Here are his impressions of the car.

The 1988 version of Ford's star performer is based on the Sapphire Ghia, and the first thing that springs to mind looking at the car is the low-key nature of its external appearance. Gone is that massive rear wing of the hatchback Cossie: this has been determined unnecessary on the Sapphire shell, which has improved aerodynamic stability compared with the normal Sierra. What is more, there are no plans to develop motorsport versions of the car. Therefore, all that is needed on the new model is a discreet bootlid spoiler. At the front of the car an integrated bumper and spoiler (after the style of, but not quite the same as that of the original Sierra Cosworth) is employed. These modifications, along with a set of purpose-designed alloy wheels, are all that set the new car apart from its lesser stablemates.

This, I feel, will be one of the main appeals of the car — many owners of the original RS Sierra have developed a painful awareness of the fact that their cars have become targets for the attentions of the police and the public alike.

The interior of the car is to full Ghia specification, with power windows and mirrors, sunroof, high-grade stereo, and all of the usual trappings. The trim is enhanced further by the inclusion of a pair of Recaro fully-adjustable seats in place of the standard front Ghia items. The RS nature of the car is hinted at by a leather-trimmed sports steering wheel and a leather-trimmed gearknob.

I found the driving position to be very comfortable for long periods at a time, the seat adjustment combinations making it possible for any driver to achieve his or her perfect position. The instrument panel appeared both comprehensive and well laid out, and the driver enjoys a good, clear view in both daylight and darkness.   ▷

ARRIVAL

The suspension is smooth and progressive, giving a ride quality which is the equal of almost any worthwhile car, yet at the same time endowing the car with exemplary roadholding capabilities: the car follows its line through a bend with deceptive ease. It is also a very forgiving car, and will even withstand being driven badly. Anti-lock brakes come as standard, and the feel of the car is so stable that it is even possible to lift or to brake in the middle of a high-speed corner without upsetting the car!

Another hint at the supremacy of this machine came when I was leaving a slippery stretch of road, and inadvertently applied a little too much power — resulting in a tail-out situation. Just a touch of opposite lock was enough to bring the car back into line, and I was away again, flying along as intended.

Acceleration is swift, to say the least — Ford claim 6.1 seconds to sixty — and the turbo starts to come in from about 2500 r.p.m. Power steadily increases, and by 3500 to 4000 r.p.m. you can feel the power really start to surge, as you are pushed gently back in the seat.

All in all, my too-brief test proves that this truly is a great car, and I was unable to find anything to fault with it.

For all of its power — and there is plenty of it, with 204 b.h.p. to be found under the bonnet — the car is surprisingly docile in traffic. The clutch pedal is light and untiring, as is the power-assisted steering with its variable rate rack system. This gives the benefit of feeling firm when travelling at speed, yet is light to use at lower speeds, on full lock.

URBANE GUERRILLA

Ford's newest supercar combines the performance of the original Cosworth with the subtle appearance of the Sapphire saloon. We put the car to the test.

By Dennis Foy.

After the Streetfighter, the outrageous RS Cosworth with its massive rear spoiler and 150 m.p.h. abilities, came the RS 500, a true world championship contender with even more musclepower backed up by yet more aggressive looks. Now, two years after the initial RS Cosworth burst onto the scene, comes the third generation of the car – but this time the aggression is muted, and the suit of clothes neatly tailored to make the car appear far more of a city slicker than its predecessors. It is no less muscular than the original RS Cosworth – the illusion is achieved by concealing everything within a subtly-altered version of the Sapphire four-door bodyshell.

Mechanically, the car is little-changed from the original three-door Cosworth. It uses the same 204 b.h.p. two-litre engine, a sophisticated twin-cam built to their own design by Cosworth Engineering, but based around the standard Pinto cylinder block. The induction system is by means of a Garrett-AiResearch T03 turbocharger, fuelled by a Weber Marelli electronic control unit which also co-ordinates the ignition and turbo boost systems. Maximum torque, which is 204 lb/ft, is achieved at 4500 r.p.m., with some 160 lb/ft being made by a mere 2300 r.p.m., and at the redline there is still 165 lb/ft being developed.

Backing up this engine is a Borg Warner close-ratio five-speed manual gearbox, identical to that used in the American Mustang ▶

It can only be a matter of time before imitations start to appear; these extra panels will fit any model of Sapphire, and could be adapted for front of current-range Sierras. ▼

URBANE GUERRILLA

◄ SVE save for a less over-driven top gear. Drive passes from there to a viscous-coupled limited slip differential with a final drive gear of 3.64:1. The LSD is smooth and progressive in its action, taking up any wheelspin neatly and effectively.

Stopping a supercar such as this is of paramount importance, and Ford have made use of disc brakes on each corner – solid at the rear, ventilated at the front – to ensure that retardation is all that it ought to be. Four-pot racing specification calipers operate the front brakes, and there is full power assistance. Just to make sure that all works as it ought to at all times, electronic anti-lock braking control is a standard fitment.

The suspension system is similarly comprehensive. At the front of the car are a pair of McPherson struts located by lower track control arms, and aided by a 28mm anti-roll bar. Concentric coil springs and twin-tube gas-filled dampers ensure that ride quality and handling standards are both equally high. At the rear of the car are a pair of mono-tube gas-filled dampers, separate coil springs, a 16mm anti-roll bar, and independent semi-trailing arms. These, along with the differential casing, all locate to a tubular subframe mounted to the body. Uniball solid joints are used in place of the usual rubber bushings in the interests of chassis sharpness, and much work has gone into the settings (a lot of which was learnt from the track activities of earlier Cosworths) of the entire suspension settings to ensure that optimum stability is retained at all times.

Much praise has been heaped upon the steering of the earlier Cosworths, for the way in which it has managed to combine lightness and responsiveness. The newcomer is no different in this respect, using the same variable-rate rack which ensures a constant feedback of information about where the front wheels are and what they are doing, without ever becoming difficult or heavy to use. The steering rack works in a most impressive manner, by varying the pitch between the rack and the pinion that drives it; as the rack turns out towards full lock, its ratio becomes sharper. This means that the wheels turn more easily, which would normally result in an increase in steering effort at the wheel. However, Ford have used a special torsion valve

which senses the attitude of the wheels and increases the hydraulic assistance to compensate.

The bodywork is basically the same as that of any other Sierra Sapphire, but with one or two little detail touches. For a start, there is a pair of rocker panel covers which have a neat concave moulding in them, and which act to help protect the ends of the central bodyshell from stones thrown up by the big Dunlop ULP tyres. Then there is the new front spoiler and bumper assembly. This is different from that of the previous Cosworth Sierras, principally because the nose section of the earlier models was based upon the first generation Sierra, which had different light clusters and nose section. Even so, the "family resemblance" is

> "The Cosworth never fails to supply the driver with information about what all four wheels and the engine are doing."

striking, particularly when the radiator grille is taken into account. On the bootlid of the car is a neat, and by RS Cosworth standards very restrained, rear spoiler. Finally, there is a set of alloy rims which are new, and purpose-designed for this model. These are somewhat less than easy to clean, and are best attacked with a power washer such as those springing up on the forecourts of rural garages.

Another substantial difference between this Cosworth and the three-door version is the standard of trim and internal

TUNING THE COSWORTH

Since the original Cosworth appeared on the scene, a number of companies have started to produce alternative componentry for the various electronic units which control the engine management system. These effectively raise the output of the engine by anything up to 175 b.h.p., and at a variety of costs which run from the suspiciously cheap to the apparently very expensive. For road use, an increase of perhaps 75 b.h.p. ought to be considered a sensible limit.

Should you purchase a Cosworth and be contemplating increasing the power outputs, it is worth talking to the various experts and discussing your aspirations with them.

USEFUL CONTACTS

Abbot Racing – Telephone: 025 587 636.
Brodie-Brittain Racing – Telephone: 0280 702389.
Mountune – Telephone: 0621 54029.

equipment. The original car was conceived primarily as a sports saloon, and as such the level of equipment was as low as it was possible to get away with, given the cost of the car. However, the four-door model is being marketed very much as a high speed businessman's express, with no intentions of the car seeing racetrack action. Consequently, the interior specification of the car is based upon that of the Ghia Sapphire, suitably upgraded by the addition of a pair of Recaro LS reclining bucket seats, a leather-trimmed steering wheel, and a leather-trimmed gearknob.

Interestingly, there are no options whatever available for the car. Ford considering that it has everything necessary as standard equipment. This includes a heated front windscreen as well as the usual heated rear glass, radio antenna integrated into the rear heater element, variable sweep on the wiper delay, power winding on all four windows, Ford's top-of-the-line stereo system with booster amplifier and six speakers, and a manual tilt-and-slide sunroof. Central locking operating from either front door, and featuring Chubb high-security locks, is another standard fitment. Finally, the car is treated to a substantially greater level of soundproofing than that enjoyed by previous Cosworth owners.

But so much for the specifications. What matters as much — if not more — is the car's ability on the road.

The car fires up instantly that the ignition key is turned, regardless of whether the car is cold or hot. It settles down immediately to a smooth and even tickover, with a deep, but restrained, burble coming from the downspout-sized exhaust tailpipe. The engine is immediately responsive to the slightest prod of its throttle pedal, but in the interests of engine longevity it would pay to let everything warm through thoroughly before actually opening the car up. For the same reasons, it is also advisable to let the engine idle for a few moments after a hard run, before switching off. This allows the turbocharger to cool whilst it is still being lubricated.

When our test car arrived it had covered 1,500 miles from leaving the factory, which meant that it was officially run in. However, the gearshift was extremely stiff and obstructive, and the clutch was less smooth than it might be, which soured our initial impressions of the car; it was virtually impossible to make steady smooth progress. Fortunately, as our ten days with the Cosworth went on, matters improved, and by the time that the car went back the clutch action was extremely progressive, and the gearshift was at the "hot knife through butter" standard that we have come to expect of the RS Cosworth.

When the roads are damp and conditions slippery, great caution must be exercised with the right foot, as too many of the 204

horses coming down the line will soon have the 205/50 Dunlop D40 tyres breaking contact with the road, and go sliding sideways. And this doesn't just happen exiting bends, either; a straight line powershift into second at high engine revs will have the back end of the car writhing like a supercharged rattlesnake. Fortunately, the suspension geometry is such that a slight decrease in power will immediately restore the car to the intended line. In fact, this characteristic became something of a plus for all who drove the car, as we played the game of hanging the tail out and catching it again in true RS tradition.

The Cosworth arrived on a wet day, and it rained again the following morning. However, the day after that was dry, and we decided to see just what it can do on fast, winding country roads. What the car can do is to make such roads feel positively

easy to negotiate at very high speeds, and I found myself pressing the car ever harder, ever deeper into tight curves, trying to get the tyres to start to sing. But every time I did this, all that happened was that the car exited the bend like it had been fired from a catapult, tyres hooked up and pressing every horsepower into the tarmac. The levels of grip that the Cosworth can achieve in dry conditions are truly awesome, and on a par with cars like the Porsche 928 and the Aston Martin Vantage. And just like those cars, when the limits of adhesion are finally approached, breakaway takes the form of a superbly-controllable four wheel drift.

SPECIFICATIONS
FORD SIERRA RS COSWORTH

ENGINE TYPE	4 cylinder DOHC	**BRAKING SYSTEM**	Teves anti-lock, all disc, servo
BORE x STROKE	90.8mm x 77mm		assisted
SIZE	1993cc	**WEIGHT**	2754 lbs
BHP @ RPM	204 @ 6000	**POWER/WEIGHT RATIO**	163 b.h.p./ton
TORQUE LB/FT @ RPM	204 @ 4500	**WHEELBASE**	102.7"
FUEL SYSTEM	Weber Marelli electronic injection,	**LENGTH**	176"
	Garrett T03 Turbocharger	**WIDTH**	75"
DRIVEN WHEELS	Rear	**HEIGHT**	53"
TRANSMISSION	5-speed manual	**TEST MILEAGE**	1,264 miles
SUSPENSION: FRONT	MacPherson struts, with anti-roll	**MANUFACTURER'S MPG**	21-23
	bar	**TEST MPG**	24.0
REAR	Independent trailing arms with	**PRICE AS TESTED**	£19,000
	anti-roll bar	**INSURANCE GROUP**	Special quotation

MANUFACTURER: Ford Motor Company, Dagenham, Essex, England.

▲Interior of the car is based on that of the Sapphire Ghia, but comes standard with Recaro seats.

◄ Such are the suspension settings of the car, that it is extremely easy to line up for a series of bends, and to make the transition from left hand to right hand curves smoothly, tidily, and without ever lurching or pitching. The big brakes bite excessively when the car is cold, but once they have warmed through their action is extremely effective, and at the same time smooth. Only in particularly adverse weather conditions is it possible to feel the anti-lock mechanism clicking into effect through the pedal. The Recaro seats do a superb job of retaining both driver and passenger whilst making rapid progress through a series of curves, and are supremely comfortable over a long journey as well. The driver's seat is height-adjustable, which means that the pilot can set the seating position to perfection, whether they be short or tall. We proved this, by having a selection of drivers from five-feet-and-half-an-inch to six-feet-four-inches tall try out the car.

Whilst control response is not quite as shiny and sharp as the Evolution-special RS 500, the saloon version of the Cosworth still never fails to supply the driver with a constant feedback of information about what all four wheels and the engine are doing, or are about to do. The steering action is nothing short of perfect, turning in cleanly, never becoming either too light or too heavy, and constantly advising of the attitude of the road

PERFORMANCE

0-30	2.24 seconds
0-60	6.09 seconds
Standing ¼ mile	14.67 seconds
Maximum speed	145 m.p.h.

N.B. All performance figures are mean, from six runs in opposite directions.

wheels. The thick leather rim of the steering wheel falls perfectly to hand, allows fingertip control of the trafficator and wiper switches, and gives adequate space to see all major instruments. Interestingly, there is no boost gauge to advise the driver of inlet tract pressures — further confirmation of Ford's intention that this machine be viewed as purely a road car.

As the figures quoted earlier suggest, the engine has a broad torque spread and is immediately responsive to the throttle pedal. However, there is still a degree of lag to contend with which means that very rapid progress along bendy roads calls for a slightly different approach to the normal: pushing deep into the bend, having scrubbed off the speed whilst in a straight line, it pays to apply the power earlier than one would in a car with a naturally-aspirated engine. That way, the power is developing fully at the point of the bend where it is needed. Failure to do this means that the car is drifting through the bend for a fraction too long. The balance of the car is very difficult to upset, and so there is rarely any danger present by not "pre-loading" the throttle — doing so merely increases the velocity at which the car can travel away from the curve.

Around town, the car is as docile as a 1.6 Sierra, quite content to potter along at thirty. But when the traffic clears, there is so much power on tap that a squeeze of the pedal is enough to have the car rocketing forward. What is more, there can be very few cars around capable of outrunning an RS Cosworth from the traffic lights. Standstill to thirty takes but two and a quarter seconds, and sixty can be achieved in as little as six seconds, with the limited slip differential seeing to it that traction is instant, even when the power is piled on. In-gear acceleration times are similarly impressive, with the highly-useable 30-50

burst through the traffic, with the car in second, taking exactly 2.7 seconds. Being very lazy on urban "A" roads and leaving the car in fifth, it is possible to run from fifty to seventy in 4.3 seconds.

Motorway behaviour of the car is impeccable, too, thanks mainly to the combination of powertrain and aerodynamics. The Sapphire bodyshell is superior to that of the Sierra hatchback in its ability to deal with crosswinds, and the additional spoilers of the Cosworth version make the car even more stable at speed, with no noticeable effects from even quite high winds coming in from the side. The car lopes along happily at all speeds, and crusing is pleasantly relaxed thanks to the additional soundproofing. It is only when the engine is

approaching its redline that noise levels become intrusive. Ride quality is never less than good, even on poor surfaces.

The Cosworth is just as useable at night as it is through the daylight hours. It is possible to adjust the brightness of the panel lamps which illuminate the instruments, and the homofocal headlamps offer a good, clean, sharp cut-off when on dip. If full beam is switched on, the range of the headlamps increases substantially, offering more than adequate light for most situations. When weather conditions are foggy, there is a pair of additional front driving lamps, and a pair of integral rear high-intensity lights. There are courtesy lights at both front and rear of the passenger area, and these are fitted with a delay facility; they stay on for twenty seconds after closing the doors, which

Difficult-to-clean wheels were specially designed for this model, and are not available on other cars in the range.▼

"Being very lazy and leaving the car in fifth, it is possible to run from 50 to 70 in 4.3 seconds."

means that there is no unnecessary fumbling about in the dark.

Given its performance and accommodation, the RS Cosworth is almost in a class of its own. It has an integrity of build that puts it on a par with BMW, and the doors open and close with a satisfying "engineered" feel. It is only the bootlid, which clatters shut like that of a Mk II Escort which has seen better days, that lets the car down.

In fact, it is from BMW that the only threat to the Cosworth's supremacy emerges. Their M5, the 286 b.h.p. version of their 5-series, is also a four door salon, and, like the Cosworth, is a subtle and understated car. The M5 is actually faster on top speed than the Ford (153 m.p.h., versus the Ford's 145 m.p.h.), and the acceleration to sixty is only slightly slower at 6.2 seconds. But there is a price to pay for the German car of £35,000 – which compares less than favourably with the £19,000 being asked for the RS Cosworth.

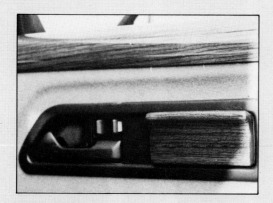

NEW TRIM ITEMS

Before the car even went on sale, Power Engineering had developed a set of trim items which improve the appearance of the Cosworth's interior. Hand-made to a standard normally only found in limousines, the set of walnut cappings are veneered in Zebrano, the same type of grain which graces the interior of top-line Mercedes models.

The complete set comprises four door cappings, rear door ashtray covers, a replacement for the ECU cover ahead of the passenger, a cover for the window switches, and a gearshift knob.

The set costs less than £400 (a real bargain, when considering the craftsmanship which goes into them), and are available from Power Engineering at Department P.F., Unit 9, Wyvern Way, Uxbridge, Middlesex UB8 2XN. Telephone: 0895 55699.

On balance Ford have produced an undoubted winner with the newcomer. It certainly delivers the claimed performance through the gears, and its actual top speed is only slightly down on the figure claimed by Ford of 149 m.p.h. The car is let down a little by the plainness of its interior, and one or two people with whom we spoke expressed concern about how the car will hold together in years to come. We have no answer to the latter matter beyond the fact that the bodyshell is guaranteed for six years, and already Power Engineering have started to produce walnut trim pieces for the interior of the car which will make it far more attractive to the eye. It can only be a matter of time before specialist trimmers offer leather upholstery for the car, which would put the interior into the level of trim that suits the overall image of the RS Cosworth – that of a very urbane machine. ●

WINNER TAKES ALL

Since its creation, Ford have re-written the rules on high-performance saloon cars with their Sierra Cosworth. First came the winged monster in 1987, followed closely by the RS 500 evolution version. Then came the urbane guerilla, the Sapphire. Now that car too has been radically revised, to become the Cosworth 4x4. **Ian Corry** has been sampling the machine — and concludes that Ford have yet another sure-fire winner on their hands.

That drive through the Spanish Pyrenees was the best run that I have ever had since I started driving. I had been given two choices when I was about to leave S'Agora for the seventy-odd mile drive to Gerona Aeroporto and the 'plane home; I could either take the same lowland route that I had driven out on the previous day when I had arrived in Cataluna or I could take the high road, up into the mountains.

I am glad that I chose the latter option, because it gave me far more of an insight into the fabulous level of grip that the latest

RS Cosworth can offer. Like all mountain routes, the straights get shorter the higher that the road climbs, and the tighter the bends become, eventually leading to a set of very demanding hairpins. The weather also got more severe as I climbed higher into the mountains, with snow and ice taking over from the

balmy February weather of the coastal resort where I and a number of colleagues had spent the previous night.

As we outlined in our March issue, the newest version of the RS Cosworth combines the driveline of the XR4x4/Granada 4x4 with a revised version of the famed, race-and-rally proven sixteen valve turbocharged twin cam engine. Externally, the new car is set apart from its predecessor by a pair of vents to allow underbonnet heat to escape, by white front indicator lenses (the bulbs are now coloured amber to meet European legislation) and by a blacked-out set of rear lights.

There are a few detail changes inside the car, as well. There is additional stowage space provided — although there is nowhere to put any compact discs, despite a CD player now being included on the list of options for the car — and there is now remote operation for the filler cap flap and for the bootlid.

Setting up for the ideal driving position is made easier still, now that the height, reach and rake adjustments of the 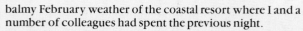 wonderfully supportive Recaro sports seats have been matched by variable reach and height control on the steering column, which is still topped off by the same thick leather-rimmed steering wheel found on previous models of Sapphire and Sierra Cosworth. Pedal spacing and weight is just as it previously was, but there is a vital difference in the other control, that for the gearchange; whereas former Cosworth owners will be familiar with the Borg-Warner transmission which used to feature in the car, the latest version has the stubby and precise MT-75 gearlever — built integrally with the gearbox, rather than being screwed in later — which is now found in virtually all of the rear and four wheel drive Ford models. This is less baulky than the old Borg-Warner lever in operation, and allows slightly quicker shifts.

The engine revisions were made primarily to improve reliability, reduce noise, vibration and harshness, and to increase the available power to compensate for the increased drag of driving through four wheels rather than just two. Firing up the machine the tickover seems smoother, and throttle response is certainly good; there is still a degree of turbo lag evident, but in all but the most demanding of situations, I found myself driving around this by keeping the engine speed up to above the turbo's boost threshold. The engine still sounds a little noisy and thrashy at very high revs, ➤

WINNER TAKES ALL

but this is less noticeable than it was on earlier examples of the Cosworth engine.

The extra sixteen brake horsepower doesn't make itself immediately apparent, but a glance at the speedometer whenever conditions allow makes it obvious that the additional power exists; the car really is extraordinarily quick once up and running.

There is more body roll than I had expected but this is never enough to upset the road wheels, which seem to track through on the intended line of a bend without any deviation. The car is staggeringly sure-footed, even on icy surfaces, the combination of four wheel drive, very carefully selected spring and damper rates, neatly-specified steering geometry and the newly-selected standard Bridgestone RE71 tyres all contributing.

Only on very tight hairpin bends does the car prove difficult to keep up on its powerband, as the very slow (relatively ...) entry speeds for the bend have the engine down to perhaps 1500 r.p.m. There is consequently a momentary lapse in power delivery until the turbocharger starts to deliver its goods. Even off-power cornering is undramatic, though, so well-sorted is the suspension system. In fact, I even tried, at a suitably safe moment, lifting off from the throttle in mid-bend to see what would happen. The result was that the body pitched a little as the springs unloaded, but the wheels never left their line.

When the ground under the car is slippery or icy, too enthusiastic a prod on the throttle pedal will have the tail of the car wagging a little, but backing off momentarily from the throttle pedal will have it slotting back into place immediately. The original two wheel drive car was idiot-proof in its handling. The new 4x4 version is everything-proof, probably one of the safest cars that I have ever tried out.

There is usually a trade-off, a degree of compromise between outright handling and roadholding, and the ride quality. Proving their supremacy at chassis design, Ford Special Vehicle Engineering have managed to endow the 4x4 RS with an excellent ride as well as with staggeringly good handling — the car soaks up the bumps and bangs thrown at it by Spanish roads (which are if anything worse than British ones) without the occupants ever feeling a thing. The Sapphire bodyshell, specially stiffened to handle the extra strain of a four wheel drive system, offers plenty of room for four adults, with enough space in the back to squeeze in an additional passenger for shorter journeys. The boot space is equal to the cabin's carrying capacity — and Ford even seem to have compensated for the additional weight of the spoiler on the bootlid by beefing up the balance springs of the hinge assembly.

The acceleration and the braking are on a par with the handling. Although the 0-60 time for the four wheel drive car is a little slower than it was in the rear wheel drive Sapphire (6.6 seconds, rather than a straight six), the difference is barely noticeable — and the total lack of wheelspin of the

THE ENGINE CHANGES

The Cosworth engine which is used in this car differs from the earlier examples in a number of ways. The cylinder block has been produced from a fresh casting mould which offers greater integral stiffness, and also helps reduce noise levels.

The head casting is also new, and is again designed to be stiffer and less prone to twisting under extremes of chamber heat. A new gasket is also used to reduce the possibilities of blowing, a common cause for complaint with owners of two wheel drive Sierra and Sapphire Cosworths.

Mahle pistons now feature in the engine, with a ring pack design aimed specifically at reducing the engine's oil consumption. An oil spray provides under-piston cooling, and the oil pump now flows more than it did previously. Ford now specify synthetic oil, rather than the previous mineral-based lubricant. The water pump has also been revised to increase coolant flow, and there is a new by-pass in the cooling system to accelerate the warming-up process and to increase heater hot airflow.

The turbocharger too has been redesigned and now features a resited wastegate actuator. Sitting on a 4-into-2-into-1 cast nickel-iron manifold, the turbo unit is watercooled, features pressure bearing lubrication, and flows through a larger intercooler than previously.

Fuelling is revised as well, the fuel rail being fed by a submerged electrical pump and the fuel rail being redesigned to improve efficiency. Fuel lines are now covered in a new fire-resistant material, and there is a separate rich-mixture device to control air supply whilst

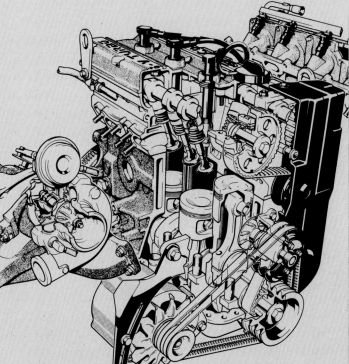

the engine is warming up.

Running at eight pounds of boost, and feeding into the sixteen-valve cylinder head, the turbocharger system is able to produce 220 b.h.p. @ 6250 r.p.m., and to give out 220 lb/ft of torque at 2500 r.p.m. — the latter figure being extremely impressive for a forced-induction engine, and one which contributes greatly to the overall driveability of the car.

The first RS car to come on sale with four wheel drive as a standard feature, the latest Sapphire features all-white finish front lights and all-black finish rear clusters.

four-by-four will compensate for that lost half second in most situations. The brakes of the original car were excellent, and the newcomer is no different — pressing the middle pedal scrubs off speed quickly and in direct proportion to the amount of weight applied.

If the car has a fault, I couldn't find it during my two test drives.

Whilst the drive through the mountains was exhilarating and exciting, and whilst it served to prove the value of the four wheel drive system when coupled to a lively and responsive development of what was already a very good engine, the previous day's drive — again of about ninety miles — had given me a chance to open up the car on longer straights.

I saw an indicated 145 m.p.h. on the speedometer during one short burst on an otherwise deserted stretch of straight road, and there was still more to come. Allowing for speedometer error (optimistic speedos are something of a Ford trademark — it has been said by one development engineer that the marketing department prefer things that way), it seems to bear out Ford's claim that the car is capable of 150 miles per hour. Ford claim that the in-motion acceleration bursts for the 4x4 are the same as those of the earlier car, and again quick (non-metered) tests seem to bear out their sentiments.

Attacking bends at the end of long, high-speed straights it is easy to set the car up for the correct line, and to swoop through and out of the other side without upsetting anybody or anything — simply point the car, slot the lever into the appropriate gear after braking, and roll on as much power as you like and the car will sail through. The term "cornering on rails" has been overworked to death in just about every magazine and by virtually every motoring writer, but it still springs to mind as the ideal description of this car's abilities.

As with all other four wheel drive Fords, the power split is biased towards the rear wheels, that axle getting two-thirds of ▶

THE TUNING POTENTIAL

A major growth industry has evolved, based around reprogramming and re-engineering RS Cosworth Sierra and Sapphire engines, and the industry is expected to carry on with the new car as soon as supplies start to make their way into the showrooms of dealerships.

The engine management system used in the 4x4 car is basically the same as that of previous cars, being a Weber-Marelli electronic control unit. This is not too difficult to reprogram by a specialist, and the various sensors and controllers are likewise easy to modify by an expert. It therefore follows that the engine can be readily persuaded to handle another few pounds of boost, resulting in perhaps three hundred horsepower without too much difficulty, and without any great loss in reliability.

Where the car is likely to have an Achilles heel is in the area of its transmission; although the flywheel has been designed to accept the full range of Motorsport clutches quickly and easily, the gearbox itself is the MT-75 which has been designed to handle no more than 275 lb/ft of torque, according to Ford's engineers at the time of the transmission's introduction. This, presumably, is why Ford Motorsport are using complete new internal gear clusters within the casing.

Because Motorsport have homologated a number of different options for the car such as bigger four-pot brakes and lower final-drive gears, these are presumably about to become available from Ford RS dealerships, and so will go onto road cars without too much difficulty. There will also presumably be optional dampers — probably from Bilstein — available to suit the new car.

WINNER TAKES ALL

the available power. For the most part the car feels like a normal rear wheel drive machine until the bend is tight and the power is on. At that point it is possible to feel the front wheels contributing their share, pulling the front of the car into line. There is never any battle between the front wheels and the steering wheel, though — whilst the driver is aware of what the front set of Bridgestones are up to, it is by a constant gentle feedback rather than by any tugging or wrenching. Steering weight itself is excellent, offering light and easy cornering and parking at very low speeds, but without every becoming "floaty" at higher speeds.

The only negative aspect of the two-day sampling session of the Sapphire 4x4 Cosworth was that I was able to try out a car in European specification, but not in the level of trim which will go on sale in Britain. This meant that I was unable to be sure of how good the car will feel in right hand drive form from the driver's seat, and of what level of equipment there will be in the British market cars. According to Ford's people at the launch in Spain, the car will be at least as well equipped as the two wheel drive car was — and possibly better. This means that such features as a sunroof, power windows, heated front screen, heated and electrically-adjustable mirrors and so forth will all be part of the standard set-up. There will also be upgraded stereo systems and leather trim available on all models, not just a few specials from selected dealerships. Priced at £24,995 the new RS Cosworth is not cheap, but from my experiences it is excellent value — there is not another car in that price range which can offer the same blend of performance, comfort, accommodation and handling. Ford are looking to the car to be a winner in rallying as well as on the road — and from my experience of the car in road form, the latter is theirs. Winner takes all? Ford have a certain winner with this car.

MOTORSPORT PLANS

The car is being homologated for competition use in its basic form, Ford being optimistic about being able to build the required five thousand examples by the deadline of August 1st, 1990. Once the five thousand have been built, Ford will then be expected to produce five hundred evolution models — although whether this will be known as the RS 500 4x4 is not certain. What is certain is that pre-production examples of what is expected to be the evolution model already exist at Ford's new Motorsport centre in Boreham. These feature six-speed Getrag transmissions, triple-selective adjustable (from on-board) damping, and 300+ b.h.p. engines.

In Group A specification, the standard car will feature a lower compression (7.2:1, rather than the standard 8.0:1) set of pistons, which will allow the boost to be increased substantially — the result being 295 brake horsepower at 6250 r.p.m., and a torque peak of 270 lb/ft of torque at 4500 r.p.m.

The bodyshells will be totally seam-welded for durability, and will have an integral steel multi-point roll cage to meet regulations. Lightweight Kevlar will be used to protect the sump and the rear axle, and both front and rear axles will have oil coolers fitted. The MT-75 transmission will have a close-ratio set of gears installed, and the clutch will be replaced by a multi-plate racing item. Final drive ratio has been set at 4.4:1 for most events, which is appreciably lower than the 3.92:1 gearing for the production car.

Uprated brakes are used, with ventilated 315mm front discs being matched by vented 285mm rear items. Four-pot calipers and an adjustable pedal box feature on the rally car — an arrangement which we can see appearing on road-going examples, as the tuners take hold of the latest Sierra Cosworth. Wheels are bigger on the competition car, with 16″ being the specified diameter, and with a choice of widths from six to eight and a half inches.

Overall weight of the car has been set at 1140 kg dry, which means that the machine will have a power-to-weight ratio of about 255 b.h.p./ton in rally trim.

THE FASTEST FIESTA YET

With the introduction of the RS Turbo, the Fiesta line-up is now complete. We have been trying the new flagship.

By Dennis Foy.

I t tingles. The new RS Turbo Fiesta — the first authentic, production Rallye Sport example of Ford's smallest car — positively tingles.

In many ways, the car reminds me of the all-white Escort RS Turbo from 1985; both cars share a similarly lively chassis, and both have a similar degree of urgency about their forward motion; press the right-hand pedal and things happen immediately. And both have a very very high fun factor. But whereas the Escort was based on a car which first put in an appearance in 1980, the Fiesta is evolved from a model range almost a decade newer — and in many ways it shows.

Externally, the car shares much of its appearance with the model it deposes from the top of the Fiesta range, the XR2i. The basic set of body panels already seen on the XR2i are carried over to the Rallye Sport car, along with the dual set of driving lamps which live below the front bumper. However, to set the car apart from its stablemate the keyline around all examples of Turbo (regardless of main

body colour) is in vivid apple green, and the six-slot wheels of the XR3i have been supplanted by a new set which have three spokes. Final distinctions between the two cars are achieved by Ford having added a neat pair of bonnet ventilation louvres, and adding the roof-height additional tailgate aerofoil onto the list of parts for colour-keying. Special decals tell the non-conversant that the car is an RS model, and that it has turbo power.

Within the car, the familiar package seen on RS cars for the last decade has been applied; the standard rear seats are still in place, but for the driver and front passenger there are now a pair of Recaros. The driver also benefits from a Sapphire Cosworth-style three-spoke leather-rimmed steering wheel, and from a leather-rimmed gearknob.

But it is beneath the Fiesta's rear-hinging bonnet that the price tag of just under £12,000 is justified, with the familiar CVH engine being treated to a Garrett AiResearch T.02 turbocharger, which boosts the power of the engine from the hundred and ten of the XR2i to a nett hundred and thirty three. But more impressive than the brake horsepower is the engine's new torque figure; this is no less than 183 Nm (some 135 lb/ft), which is achieved at a mere 2800 r.p.m. — and from the feel of the car that figure holds good right around to the fast side of five and a half thousand revs per minute.

Much of the reason for the car's power level and performance is attributable to the choice of turbocharger for the powerplant. In order to achieve that level of torque at such a low engine speed, the decision was taken to utilise the diminuitive T.02 unit, which spins up to positive boost extremely quickly and which will feed as much air as the engine is likely to need right through to the vehicle's redline of more than six thousand revs.

A smaller turbine unit will limit top-end performance in ➤

The car has evolved from the XR2i. External identification is achieved by spotting the three-spoke wheels, bonnet louvres and colour-keyed rear spoiler.

THE FASTEST FIESTA YET

FORD PHOTOGRAPHIC UNIT

the aftermarket as that system has proven notoriously difficult to break into, and to reprogramme.

The car makes use of a modified cooling system when compared with the rest of the range of Fiestas, in order to control the greatly increased heat generated by the turbocharger installation. Close scrutiny of the car's front bumper moulding shows that there is a slight detent now moulded in, which allows clearance for the front-mounted cooling fan; this is used in place of the more usual fan found behind the radiators of more mundane Fiestas. Air is extracted from beneath the bonnet by those neatly designed bonnet venting louvres, and as might be expected, an air-to-air intercooler is integrated into the nose of the car to cool the pressurised air before it enters the engine after leaving the turbocharger.

The transaxle of the Turbo Fiesta is shared with that of the Escort Turbo, although as was mentioned previously, there is no viscous coupling. Final drive is the familiar 3.82:1 assembly, and the interim gearing differs from that of the rest of the Fiesta range by having a closer-set range of gears with a direct 1:1 fourth gear; all of the other Fiestas have an overdriven fourth. Top gear too differs, the 0.76:1 of the rest of the range being replaced by a slightly "shorter" 0.80:1. The clutch assembly of the car is the same 220mm driven plate diameter as that of the rest of the 1600cc Fiestas.

The absence of a viscous coupling is nothing like as detrimental to the car's on-road behaviour as might be expected, thanks primarily to the well sorted suspension system. Again this is carried over from the XR2i, but with a degree of fine tuning to suit the characteristics of the forced-induction engine. The front springs are carried straight over from the less powerful car, as is the L-bar three-point bottom linkage on each strut. The struts themselves, though, have extension valving which uprate that part of their function by 15%; compression rates are unchanged. At the rear of the car the spring rates have been

Extremely sharp throttle response is achieved by down-sizing turbocharger to T.02 from more usual T.03 Garrett unit.

◄ that it will not feed sufficient amounts of air at very high pressures, but will be adequate for road use where no more than ten pounds of boost is required. It will be interesting to see just how far the aftermarket will take the car in time to come; the concensus amongst Ford's engineers is that the T.02 will allow a peak power output of perhaps a hundred and sixty brake horses, and to get the unit to develop more power it will be necessary to increase the size of the turbocharger unit to perhaps a T.03.

Unlike the "white hot" Escort Turbo from the Mk III line-up, the RS Fiesta has been conceived purely as a road car — there are no plans whatsoever for a factory-backed competition series involving the newest Fiesta. That attitude accounts for the choice of turbocharger — and also accounts for the car having a free differential unit; hitherto, all Ford series-production turbocharged cars have come with limited slip viscous couplings, to optimise traction in racing and rallying conditions. But I'm racing ahead of myself a little — back to the engine.

The powerplant for the engine is not identical to that of the RS Turbo Escort, although both engines share the same cylinder block, crankshaft and piston assemblies. The head and part of the intake plenum of the XR2i is used on the Fiesta Turbo unit, and the turbocharger sits on a specially-developed manifold which tucks the blower unit neatly into the block — overall width of the engine is the same as that of the XR2i, which has enabled Special Vehicle Engineering to utilise many of the Fiesta's standard engine bay ancilliaries. To control the fuel and ignition systems, the Fiesta becomes the first turbocharged Ford production car to make use of the EEC-IV engine management computer; this too may cause problems for increased by 20%, an anti-roll bar of 20mm diameter has been added, and the ride height has been lowered by ten millimetres. Naturally, the damping has been modified to suit the revisions in springing. A new faster-action steering rack (3.75 turns from lock to lock, rather than the former 4.2:1) has been installed at the front of the car, and the geometry has been altered to reduce camber and castor. A slight increase in toe-out has been specified, and the nett result of these amendments is to reduce the understeer of the XR2i quite substantially, to sharpen up steering response, and to give the car an altogether more crisp feel.

Another integral part of the suspension system is the choice of tyres. As with the Cosworth 4x4, Ford have taken the unusual step of specifying only one tyre type for the car, but whereas the rubber of the Cosworth is supplied by Bridgestone, the Fiesta's alloy rims are surrounded by Pirelli products. The rims themselves are 14" x 5½", and the tyres are 185/55 R 14 V P600s.

Repeating their operation from last autumn, Ford had chosen Ulster as the venue for the launch of the new car — and just like last time, the weather was bouncing rain interspersed with fine drizzle. If the car had a weakness, then these conditions would highlight it!

What became apparent within a few minutes of leaving the car park at Aldergrove Airport was that the route this year would be appreciably more demanding than that used in 1989; much of the running was on tight and twisting narrow roads — the sort that are but a fine line on the page of the Michelin Atlas covering that corner of Ireland — and there were even a couple of hillclimb sections which are a regular feature on the Circuit of Ireland. My initial reaction to the car, whilst driving at a sedate pace in traffic, was that the ride quality was firm — although not quite rock-solid — and that the steering was sharp. The Recaro seating is supremely comfortable, and unlike the seating found in Escort Turbo models, does not have the intrusive side bolsters which are constantly being caught by the driver's left elbow every time that a shift is made into second or fourth gear. The dinky steering wheel is ideally-sized for the car, and the ergonomics are so good that the driver is able to immediately feel at home in the driver's seat of the machine.

Leaving the main road and darting off onto what would be the first of a series of interesting smaller byways, I was able

to roll in some power and thrust the diminuitive machine forwards. Reaction time is instant; prod the throttle and the car scurries towards the horizon. Throwing the car into the first bend, it becomes immediately obvious why such firm springing is a feature of the turbocharged Fiesta because the device slips into, and then out of, the deviation without a hint of rolling or pitching. Uncharacteristically, I found myself virtually ignoring the quadrant tachometer's fast-moving needle, and instead made sharp upshifts based on the messages coming in via my ears and the seat of my pale grey trousers; such is the torque spread of the engine, that technique seemed to work ideally on those twisting roads.

The forced-induction CVH engine has an extremely rapid response, and progress becomes a series of ''whop-whop-whops'' as each gear up the range is grabbed, used and replaced; the clutch action is light and precise, and the same applies to the stubby (by front wheel drive standards) gear lever. The acceleration can be summed up in one word — punchy.

By decreasing the steering rack's ratio from that found on all other Fiesta models, Ford have increased the sharpness of response, doing away with much of the arm-twirling that existing Fiesta owners will be familiar with. The downside to this is that the physical inputs required by the driver have increased; at parking speeds the wheel effort is higher (although still less than that experienced on current model Escorts), but at moderate road speeds the amount of input required is still not excessive. On that first stretch of backroad north of Antrim, I had a nagging doubt or two about the steering geometry, feeling that the car was a little nervous and jiggly especially over less-than-smooth surfaces. However, as I settled into more of a rhythm I ➤

STUDIO COLLINS

THE FASTEST FIESTA YET

and has a far sharper response and pulse time than the earlier applications of the mechanical system. Although brake pedal feel was a little on the spongey side (an accepted side-effect of the ALB system), its action was still positive when in use.

Most front wheel drive cars suffer from some torque steer, but this particular machine is better than many; only pumping through patently exaggerated amounts of power will provoke the car into going sideways and not forwards — and as might be expected, the syndrome is more apparent when the road surface is wet. The condition never becomes problematic, and is easiest overcome by making a rapid upshift into second gear, then holding the power down to a sensible level.

On the subject of the gears, whilst the clusters found within the RS Turbo transaxle are closer spaced than those of lesser Fiestas, they feel slightly inconsistent; first and third are usefully long, but second and fourth could do with being about 10% taller; there is a "hole" on the upshift into fifth, but second is used and gone before you know about it.

On more open roads, it is possible to start to exploit the car's top-end range, and very impressive it is too; as speeds increase then so the downforce provided by the aerodynamics come into play, and even at figures in excess of three digits (the car will pull to more than 130 m.p.h., remember) the 2000 lb machine feels solid; the impression is of a car which weighs appreciably more. By those sorts of speeds the straight ahead steering weighting has increased, but never to the point of feeling stodgy.

The coast road which I was following at that point was like a roller coaster track, with a series of inconsistently spaced humps and ridges. On such surfaces — and at high speed — the car bounced and jolted perhaps a shade too much for comfort, but its straight line stability was unimpaired by the undulations. Only after cresting one of the rises and then going straight into a sweeping curve did the car

◄ discovered that what was happening was that I was over-reacting to each bend of the road; letting the car do a little more of the work took the twitchiness out of the nose of the Turbo, allowing a far tidier line to be achieved on each deviation from the straight and narrow.

As with any powerful front wheel drive car, care needs to be exercised when exiting a particularly tight corner or the inside wheel will spin and scramble for grip; this is the first production Fiesta which needs such respect. The turn-in action of the front wheels is as sharp as a Swann Morton No. 10a scalpel, and the car will unsteer with equal precision. Make judicious use of the throttle — not overcooking it when appropriate — and the car will reward the driver by handling smoothly, flatly and evenly. Typical of Ford's front wheel drive products, the overall balance of the newest Fiesta is towards gentle understeer, but to a far lesser degree than with, for instance, the current RS Turbo Escort; in fact it is possible, by easing off the throttle on tighter curves, to provoke a mild oversteer with the rear-end of the car easing out from the line set by the front pair of Pirellis. It would, however, take some seriously lunatic behaviour to actually provoke a spin-out.

On paper, Ford's decision to carry the braking system straight over to the newcomer from the XR2i might have seemed a little suspect, smacking of penny-pinching; yet despite serious provocation I found it virtually impossible to generate any fading from the big front discs. However, when one of the wheels was on a slightly loose surface (such as on the coastal stretches of the test route, where gravel has blown onto the inland edge of the road), the anti-lock braking system would engage a shade earlier than necessary. The anti-lock mechanism itself worked well,

Interior of the car is trimmed in a Benetton-designed fabric. Front seats are by Recaro, and the wheel and gearknob are leather-rimmed. Subtle "Turbo" legend on wheel main spoke gives game away.

display anything other than precise handling; because the suspension had temporarily unloaded and because the curve was on a stretch of road with adverse camber, I found the car wandering outwards, in a gentle drift. A brief — and very gentle — input through the steering wheel restored the status quo almost immediately.

On the straighter and more even stretches of that road, I was able to explore the upper reaches of the white machine's performance — and rapidly drew the conclusion that Ford's claim of a hundred and thirty miles per hour is by no means exaggerated; it will do it with an accomplished flair. Unfortunately, as speeds increase then so do engine noise levels — additional soundproofing on the bulkhead would be a definite advantage, as most of the noise comes from the top end of the CVH engine which sounds discordantly "thrashy" when extended beyond five thousand revs per minute. This is a situation common to all CVH-engined cars, whether they are from Ford or from the smaller independents who draw on Ford's Power Product Division for methods of propulsion, and so the Fiesta is by no means alone in being the butt of such criticism.

What also soon becomes apparent is that the car still feels like a true RS model, with messages coming back to the driver from the steering wheel rim, from the pedals and through the cushion of that supportive and comfortable Recaro driver's seat; those special sensations are still as strong in high speed cruising mode as they are when punching the model hard along twisty roads.

The machine is both quick and fast, and delivers everything that its ample specification suggests it ought; with a sprint to sixty taking seven and a half seconds, the dash to a hundred taking a mere twenty seconds, and the standing quarter mile being covered in sixteen seconds, the car can cut it with the big boys — and is able to take on virtually all comers in its own class of superheated hatchback. It also seems that the machine will be affordable to run.

At £11,950 in standard form the car is not cheap, but neither is it unduly expensive when compared with the Peugeot 205-1.9i, or the Renault 5 GT Turbo; although more costly to purchase than the latter it will outrun it (especially in the upper reaches) and also feels appreciably more solid and well constructed. As with those other two cars — which are the Fiesta RS Turbo's natural rivals —

insurance will not come cheap, and for the under 25s may prove difficult to find. But then given the levels of performance on tap, and the monopolistic nature of motor insurers in Europe, this is hardly surprising. In all other respects, the car ought to be economical with its expected average mileage of twenty six miles to each gallon of low-octane unleaded petrol, and with its minimal servicing requirements; the EEC-IV management system effectively takes away the need to recalibrate fuelling and ignition when the car is in for service which reduces maintenance times — and thus costs.

In terms of what you actually get for your money, the RS Turbo is reasonably well equipped. There are those Recaro seats, along with the leather-rimmed wheel and gearknob, but in all other respects the machine will be totally familiar territory to owners of high-series Fiesta models; the entire fascia, right down to its Premium Sound 2005 stereo radio cassette unit with four speakers, is identical to that of the XR2i. Power windows, central locking and a remote tailgate release (which only works when the ignition is switched off …) feature, along with the Fiesta's special tilt-or-remove sunroof. The Benetton-designed Ascot fabric which features on the seat facings and door panels is neatly offset by plain grey velour and vinyl, and the overall effect is pleasing and subtle.

Stowage for loose items is reasonable, if not copious; there is a pair of door pockets of modest proportions, and there is a pair of aircraft-style lockets in the front seat-backs. A cubby ahead of the front passenger is augmented by another close to the driver's right knee, and there is a small slot in the centre "console" which will just about hold twenty Benson & Hedges and a Zippo lighter. The ▶

PERFORMANCE

0-30	2.7 seconds
0-60	7.6 seconds
0-100	20.1 seconds
Standing ¼ Mile	16.1 seconds @ 88 m.p.h.
Maximum Speed	130 m.p.h.

THE FASTEST FIESTA YET

characterised the best of the Rallye Sport cars. Acceleration is sparkling — although there will always be those who want a little more oomph — and its cornering abilities are at the very top of the class. The device is rewarding to drive, and yet safe with it; it would take a seriously gung-ho attitude to get the car seriously out of shape. The car feels very "together", and despite its hard (but not to the point of shaking out the editorial fillings) ride, it felt solid and substantial. Panel fit is excellent and every one of the dozen or so examples which I have so far seen — including some in dealership showrooms — has displayed consistent and accurate seams and shut lines. It looks as though it will hold together for years to come.

The Fiesta Turbo is a true RS car. It is a serious little driving machine which is aimed fairly and squarely at the enthusiastic driver, and those of a wimpish disposition need not apply to join the small but select group of owners. As with all RS cars it will be of limited production status, and that alone will probably be enough to ensure its success. ●

◄ complement is completed by a lidded glovebox which has no lock. What is sorely lacking is somewhere worthwhile to store cassettes without having them hurtle around the inside of the glovebox, creating rattles in an otherwise rattle-and-squeak-free environment. A small, but nevertheless irritating, omission.

What is also conspicuous by its absence is anti-lock braking as a standard issue item; the much-improved Lucas Girling-Ford developed Stop Control System is available for the car, but only as a £435 option. This is at odds with the other two RS cars on sale from Ford, both of which come with anti-lock brakes as standard. Presumably the listing of this most useful and praiseworthy feature as an extra is a part of the policy of keeping the list price of the car itself to the underside of twelve thousand pounds. There are only two other options available for the car, one being the £125 rapid de-icing heated windscreen, and the other being the paint finish; in keeping with a Ford tradition te car is available only in four colours, with the plain Diamond White or Radiant Red schemes being joined by either Black or metallic Mercury Grey — the latter two costing an additional £175. One feature which is thrown in for free on the latest RS which is unavailable on all other Fiestas is that the rear side windows open. These are hinged at the leading edges, and lock open on their trailing edges to an angle of about 15°.

So in summary, what will the purchaser of the new Fiesta Turbo get in return for more than £12,500, which is what it will cost with the desirable extras?

Fun is very high on the list. The car delivers its performance with the adrenalin rush which has

SPECIFICATIONS

ENGINE TYPE
Transverse four cylinder inline SOHC
BORE x STROKE
80mm x 79.5mm
SIZE
1596cc
BHP @ RPM
133 @ 5500
TORQUE LB/FT @ RPM
135 @ 2400
FUEL SYSTEM
Ford EEC-IV electronic ignition, Garrett T.02 turbocharger
DRIVEN WHEELS
Front
TRANSMISSION
5-speed manual transaxle
SUSPENSION, FRONT
MacPherson strut independent, L-arm lower links, 16mm anti-roll bar
SUSPENSION, REAR
Torsion beam, outboard coil springs, 20mm anti-roll bar, twin-tube dampers
BRAKING SYSTEM
Front ventilated discs, rear discs, dual circuit, servo assisted, optional mechanical anti-locking system
WEIGHT
2004 lbs
POWER/WEIGHT RATIO
141 b.h.p./ton
WHEELBASE
96.3"
LENGTH
149.6"
WIDTH
64"
HEIGHT
52.2"
TEST MILEAGE
240 miles
MANUFACTURER'S MPG
25.9
PRICE AS TESTED
£12,510
INSURANCE GROUP
7
MANUFACTURER
Ford Motor Company, Dagenham, Essex

Afterword: the RS Fords and the future

The Rallye Sport marque seems set to continue into the nineties, following the same formula which has served it so well through the previous decades; and as with previous generations of RS cars, the Escort will be right there at the front of the queue.

The CE-14 series of Escorts (known outside Ford as the MarkV models) are already on sale, but at the time of writing the RS variants have yet to join in the fray; the original on-sale date has been put back yet again and is looking as though it will arrive in the spring of 1992.

The first model resurrects a name already familiar, that of RS2000. It does, however, have one vital addendum, and that is the additional nomenclature of 16v. The engine choice for the new RS two, as it will affectionately be known, is the 1-4 dual overhead camshaft unit developed by Ford for the Sierra and Granada ranges, but sporting a cylinder head with twice as many valves as previously found within that powerplant's cylinder head. This feature, combined with a revised engine management system, is sufficient to raise the power output to a respectable 150 brake horsepower, with a similar feet-poundage of torque — enough to ensure that the car will meet its prime opponent, the Astra GTE from General Motors, head-on. The power level is appreciably higher than that other traditional hot Escort competitor, the Golf GTi-16v, which can boast only 132PS.

To handle this amount of power through a front wheel drive chassis, the RS2000-16v features a much-improved suspension layout when compared to the standard CE-14 Escort: a greater diameter anti-roll bar features at the front of the car, along with 37% uprated spring and damper rates, and there is power-assisted steering as standard. At the rear, the springs and dampers are 21% stiffer than those of a standard Escort.

To complement the uprated suspension package, and to minimise sidewall distortion which can affect handling, the tyres specified for RS2000-16v are 195/50VR15 items, wrapping around a new design of 15" x 6" aluminium alloy wheels.

Because of the power levels being developed by the new engine, a completely new transaxle — the MTX-75 — has been specified for the RS2000-16v. This draws on the technology already in use with the MT-75 inline transmission, in that it has such details as cold-formed synchroniser rings, with syncromesh on every gear including reverse, and has a shift mechanism supported on roller bearings. This ought to guarantee not only a long service life, but also a smooth, precise and suitably fast gearchange mechanism. The power capacity of the MTX-75 is 270Nm, which in imperial terms is 200ft.lb of torque.

To ensure that the car will stop as well as it ought — a gripe which RS owners have mentioned in the past — the new car has electronic anti-locking, and discs on each corner. This makes it the first factory-built Escort RS to have such equipment, and finally drags the company into line with its competitors who have been using rear discs for some time.

Another complaint from RS owners has been the quality of lighting — there has been a healthy aftermarket trade in uprated headlamp bulbs. To avoid such criticisms being levelled against the RS2000-16v, a pair of high-power driving lamps are integrated into the main headlamp clusters, in much the same way as on the Cosworth Sierra models. Additional driving lamps feature in the front spoiler, just inboard of the trafficator lenses.

Mindful of comments from some quarters that the RS models were not sufficiently different either in appearance or in trim and equipment levels, there has been a concerted effort within Ford to raise the profile of the new car and to make it wholly distinctive when parked alongside other, lesser Escorts. The first feature is a front spoiler incorporating a neat aerofoil made from a soft, rubbery material. A pair of side-skirt extensions are featured over either sill, and there is extensive colour-coding: the front and rear bumpers, side skirts, mirror heads, wrapover tailgate spoiler and grilled air intake are all painted to match the main body colour.

Another distinction between this and other Escorts is the pair of raised 'bumps' on each side of the bonnet's centreline; these are essential, rather than merely cosmetic, as they compensate for the fact that the ends of the engine camshaft cover protrude above the bonnet of the car! This engine was designed for use in the Sierra and Granada bodyshells and is a tall powerplant. In an inline application this is not problematic, but when the unit is turned around and dropped into the nasal cavity of a much lower-bonneted car, then something has to give.

The car's interior specification is up to the expected standards, with a sports steering wheel, additional warning lights, and a pair of Recaro front seats. Trim fabrics are expected to be dedicated to the RS model, and once again it is likely that the range of available colours will be limited to three or four shades. Only Ford can turn parsimony into exclusivity...

The performance levels of the RS2000-16v promise to be exciting, with the 0-60 time to be in the 7.5 seconds bracket (on a good, dry surface with a suitably grippy set of tyres) and the top speed to be in the region of 140mph.

However, if it is top-level excitement that you crave, then the one to really go for is the RS Cosworth Escort.

In a peculiar sort of way, this car is a spiritual successor to the ill-fated RS1700T project: the new car is essentially an amalgamation of the very best of the Sapphire Cosworth 4x4, wrapped up in the latest Escort bodyshell, suitably altered to fit. Just as in much the same way the RS1700T was the old RS1800-style package clothed in the next generation of bodyshell...

But there the similarities end.

The Cosworth Escort is likely to become a reality for two very good reasons. The first is that the Chairman of Ford of Britain has already gone on record as saying that there will be Cosworth derivatives of all the model lines by the middle of the nineties. To renege on that promise would be act of sheer folly. The other, more substantial reason is that Ford will need a serious competition car to replace the Sierra Cosworth, which is due to cease production by the spring of 1992.

The RS Cosworth Escort is a four wheel drive machine which for motive power makes use of the same YB Cosworth turbocharged sixteen valve engine already in service in the Sapphire. Unlike the rest of the Escort range the Cosworth engine is fitted inline — a fact which caused major problems for the design team at SVE, as did also the matter of accommodating a wider track than that of the standard Escort.

The result is a special floorpan which will house the driveline in exactly the same arrangement as that already found inside the Sapphire bodyshell: strategic stiffening points have been integrated, to cope with the additional stresses brought about by the inline engine and by the rear axle arrangement.

The problem of accommodating the wider track is accomplished by widening the front and rear wings, much as Eric Zakowski did on his Escorts and Capris back in the seventies. On the pre-production prototypes these were aluminium pressings, but only time will tell if that particular design feature is carried over to the finished production model. More likely, the showroom cars will be all steel, with aluminium being reserved for special factory lightweight competition vehicles.

A massive whaletail rear spoiler (a delete option for those who prefer to maintain a lower profile) is a feature of the car, as are a pair of teardrop-shaped bonnet vents. Special sixteen-inch diameter, seven-inch wide wheels are also expected as standard.

What Ford are aiming to achieve with the RS Cosworth Escort is a car which has all the dynamics of the Sapphire Cosworth — a car which is only now starting to prove its worth as a serious rally tool — in a lighter, more compact, more aerodynamic package. Initial forays on the test track already show the package to be on target for a string of international successes in rallying — although as Ford of Britain Motorsport supremo Peter Ashcroft once observed: "Stick a number on the side and something magical happens," meaning that until the car is actually out on an event, nobody can accurately predict the outcome. It does promise, though, to be capable of taking on the best of the competition.

By producing the car as a regular showroom model, Ford will also be able to claim a new flagship, again restoring the RS Escort to the top of the tree. A four wheel drive car, laden with luxury features and with stunning performance (expect 10% better acceleration and a 10% higher top speed than the RS Sapphire 4x4), is truly the nineties answer to the first of the RS Escorts, the RS1600.

As for the remaining models in the Ford line-up, the RS Fiesta is expected to be upgraded in the foreseeable future to gain a twin camshaft, sixteen valve engine which will increase its power accordingly. The future for an RS model of Sierra is less certain, though.

The RS Cosworth came about almost by default, as a successor to the all-conquering Escorts of the seventies; then Director of Motorsport Stuart Turner axed the RS1700T programme and diverted attention to the Sierra when it was decided that the MkIII Escort would never be able to match the achievements of its predecessor. Out of that motorsport programme — essential as a marketing tool — was born the RS Cosworth as a road car, and its evolution into a four wheel drive machine with impeccable road manners was directly attributable to the needs of the Motorsport department.

But now, with the Escort poised to restore honour to the name, the need to develop an RS variant of the Sierra is much diminished: any RS car which appears in the next generation of Sierras will be there simply because Ford's marketing people feel that it will not only sell on its own account, but that it will also act as a magnet, attracting less ambitious Sierra owners into the showrooms.

But stranger things have been known to happen...

The one range which, according to Ford sources, will never have an RS model is the Scorpio. This range is pitched at the executive buyer and has already gained a Cosworth 24v variant which has most carefully been distanced from the RS end of the market. A shame, that, because a twin turbocharged version of the wonderful Cosworth V6 quad-camshaft engine, allied to a manual transmission and four wheel drive, would be the definitive big RS model. Now, how do we go about persuading Ford's marketing people that such a car would not only sell, but would elevate their street credibility to previously unattained heights?